Overcoming
Roadblocks to Success

Catherine M White

DISCLAIMER AND/OR LEGAL NOTICES:

The information presented herein represents the view of the author as of the date of publication. Because of the rate with which conditions change, the author reserves the right to alter and update her opinion based on the new conditions. The report is for informational purposes only. While every attempt has been made to verify the information provided in this report, neither the author nor her affiliates/partners assume any responsibility for errors, inaccuracies or omissions. Any slights of people or organizations are unintentional. If advice concerning legal or related matters is needed, the services of a fully qualified professional should be sought. This report is not intended for use as a source of legal or accounting advice. You should be aware of any laws which govern business transactions or other business practices in your country and state. Any reference to any person or business whether living or dead is purely coincidental.

CONTENTS

Acknowledgements

My life has been an incredible journey of trials and triumphs that have shaped me into the person that I am today. There have been many roadblocks I have faced and wished I could have surpassed, but each time I have looked back I have realized the blessings of those challenges, and I feel an immense amount of gratitude for the growth they have brought me.

I want to thank God for guiding my path all along the way, for inspiring me to be a better person today than I was yesterday, and for giving me an insatiable desire to continue to grow and the drive to keep going when it would have been so easy to give up.

I thank my courageous mother, Rachel Kendall, for the incredible example of strength she has shown me as she raised eight children on her own while pursuing a college degree. Despite the tremendous trials she faced, she never gave up, and her faith in the Lord never wavered.

I thank my four children, Shala, Austin, Braeden, and Liam (and my 'other' daughter, Wendy Suzanne) for being a part of my family, for accepting my many mistakes as a parent, and for loving me. You are the joy and light of my life. I love you with all my heart, and I thank God for trusting me to be your mother.

I thank my dear friend, Megan Martineau, for weathering many storms with me and for the brainstorming calls at the crack of dawn to help me get unstuck. You have been a big contributor to my success!

I thank the many mentors and coaches who have assisted, encouraged, and pushed me to not just follow my dreams but to build them BIG. You have given me the confidence necessary to accomplish anything I desire.

I thank my wonderful world of friends and family. Because I have been so immensely blessed with many, it would take up far too many pages to list you individually; however, I want each of you to know how important you are to me. You each have played an integral role in my life, and I will forever be grateful for you.

I compile this book with much love and gratitude for all of you!

Introduction

Helping others find success is a great passion of mine; helping others overcome the roadblocks they face during their journey to success is an even deeper passion because of the challenge it brings – and I enjoy a challenge!

Most people have a dream of doing something incredible with their lives, yet the majority of them don't take the necessary steps to pursue their passion or they give up too quickly and settle into accepting an average life, or for some, a life of misery filled with complaints for what they want and don't have.

As I have watched countless individuals give up on their dreams and many more who have never begun because of fear of failure or a limited belief that they can achieve them, I have been inspired to reach out and make a difference.

I compiled this book as a tool to help those with a desire to create success to take action toward their dreams and to stay the course amid the roadblocks they may come up against – and there will be many! It's very easy for those of you who may be starting out on your path to success to look at those who are already successful and think that there is some magic secret to obtaining success and then wonder why it's so easy for another while it's so difficult for you. The truth is, success is not easy, and there is no magic formula, but there are many strategies that you can follow to get the results you wish.

Within the following pages of this book, you will find true stories of real people who began with little more than a desire, who have traveled down a long bumpy road and have pushed through numerous obstacles to get to where they are today. With each message, you will find valuable tips that you may apply to your situation as you follow your dreams to help you get over the hurdles and push through the roadblocks.

Before you read further, one critical message I would like to leave with you is the cold hard truth that you will never get to a point in your life or business where you no longer have obstacles. Obstacles will always be there. They may be different in shape, form, or appearance, but they will always show up. You cannot run from them, but you can gain the knowledge of how to approach them in a way that they will have a lesser impact and you can use them for learning and growth.

Do not let obstacles deter you; do not let fear paralyze you; do not let mistakes discourage you. As Albert Einstein so brilliantly stated, "You never fail until you stop trying."

Enjoy your reading and be sure to glean the useful tools provided in each of the following passages.

Here's a toast to your success!

The interviews contained in this book are available by audio at: http://www.lifeleadersinternational.com/.

CHAPTER 1

Successful people do what unsuccessful people are unwilling to do.
~ Jeff Olson

I remember a time when I was at a social gathering with a group of friends. Each person was responsible for bringing a food item to share for a pot-luck meal. Someone brought a box of donuts and I wanted a taste – just enough to satisfy me – I wasn't interested in eating the whole donut because I was in really good shape and I worked hard to stay in shape. (I was taking a nutritional supplement daily, I only occasionally consumed sugary or fatty foods, and I was exercising a minimum of three hours a week. I would get up at 4:30 in the morning to work out before getting my children up for school. As a single mother, from the moment the children were up until late at night when I went to bed, my days were usually busy non-stop with working a full-time job, helping the children with homework, preparing dinner, keeping up with the laundry, dishes and other housework, running the children to their various activities, and anything else that came up, so early mornings were the best time for me to ensure I maintained a routine of regular exercise.) I cut off a quarter piece of a donut. As I picked up the small piece of donut and put it in my mouth, a heavy-set lady looked at me and said, "You don't need to worry about what you eat, you are already thin." I thought to myself, "I am thin BECAUSE I am careful about what I eat." It had not occurred to her that it took hard work to have the physique I had.

So many people look at success with a similar mentality. They expect it to come easily and when it doesn't they get frustrated, upset and give up. They then tell themselves stories like they aren't cut out for it, they don't have the right luck, they weren't destined for success, they weren't meant to be wealthy, and so on…and when they see others with success they become envious and sometimes even spiteful. We all have access to success; we all have the ability to do great things with our lives. It is our individual responsibility to take action and take the steps necessary to create our success.

I used to frequently attend activities for single adults. My favorite events were dances (I love dancing – it is my most enjoyed extra-curricular activity). Who I danced with wasn't important to me, what mattered was that I was having fun. I would go out and dance during nearly every song that played, sometimes with a group of several friends and other times one-on-one with a partner. Often I would receive comments of envy from other women because the men didn't ask them to dance yet I was always out on the dance floor having a great time and being asked to dance by the men. What they failed to realize was why I was always on the dance floor and how I became the person that got asked to dance. I was on the dance floor because I made a choice to be out on the dance floor. I was determined to dance, so I made sure I found a way to get out and do it; often that meant I went to the men and asked them to dance rather than waiting around to be asked. Because I made the initial connection, I created the opportunity to develop a friendship and then the men knew me and were comfortable with me so they would then ask me to dance. This was my secret to finding success on the dance floor.

Success begins with a desire and a will followed by action. I learned at an early age that if I want something, I have to go out and get it. If I just sit around and wait for it to come to me, it likely won't come – and if it does, it probably won't turn out the way I want. I am the only one in charge of my life and what I get from it – so it is up to me to be intentional in choosing what I want and then take action to get it.

Growing up, I lived very poorly. Up until I was ten years of age, my father was the financial supporter of our family of seven children, and he struggled at keeping a job. My siblings and I usually wore way out-of-fashion, hand-me-down clothing (occasionally we had something new that was handmade by my mother); we mainly lived off the food we grew and canned ourselves; at times we lived without plumbing and electricity. My parents had a rocky relationship, and when I was ten years old, and my mother was expecting child number eight, my parents separated. All my siblings and I lived with my mom from that point on. We went on welfare, and my mom received housing assistance, food stamps, and medical support through the state to support the family. My mother had a friend who would invite us over at times for my mom to do some housecleaning to earn some money to help cover bills and food. Often, while my siblings went off to play, I would help my mom clean, and her friend would give me some cash of my own. It was exciting for me to have my own money to spend. I couldn't wait to be twelve so I could take jobs in babysitting. As the oldest girl in my family with five of my siblings being younger than me, I gained a lot of great experience in taking care of children. Once I turned twelve, I walked around and posted flyers throughout our apartment complex to solicit my services as a babysitter. When I was thirteen, my younger sister was offered an opportunity to take over a paper route. The paper route was originally designed for someone with a car and covered too large of an area for an eleven-year-old child to cover on foot so she asked me to split the route with her. While the other children our age were sound asleep in their warm, cozy beds, my sister and I would get up at four-thirty in the morning, seven days a week, to deliver paper – rain, shine, or snow. We had some pretty severe winters at that time and would trudge through deep snow to deliver the papers. We each walked alone going sep-arate directions to best effectively cover the full route. The money I earned between the babysitting and paper route left me feeling pretty rich. I then began to buy my clothing, and I loved that I was able to choose what I wore. I also spent my money to go out with my friends and for anything else that I wanted and most of what I needed aside from food and shelter. By the time I was sixteen and old enough to have a 'real' job, I pounded the pavement and applied for any job I was eligible for and had the means to travel to. When I began making the 'big bucks' I would often spend my money on my family to do things we couldn't afford to do, such as taking my younger siblings to the carnival. It brought me joy to be able to share experiences with my siblings that they wouldn't have otherwise had.

To everyone, success is different. It is up to each of us to determine what success means for us individually – no one else can decide that for us. For me, success means having the time, money and freedom to impact the lives of others and ultimately change the world. It has been my dream to change the world for as long as I can remember. As a little girl, I had a tendency to reach out with compassion to others who were 'different' and didn't have many friends, and I would befriend them. A large reason for doing this probably came from the insecurity and shyness I had as a child, but there was more to it than that. I wanted to make them feel good; I wanted them to know they were special and important. I was in the seventh grade when I consciously began to realize the difference I wanted to make in the lives of others. I had taken a speech class as an elective requirement (this is a huge feat for a shy person). I still remember how nerve-wracking it was to stand in front of the room to give a speech. Some students had difficulty keeping their speeches within the allotted time frame; not me. I had difficulty making mine stretch long enough to meet the minimum requirement. Although I would practice and time myself beforehand, when I stood up in front of the classroom with trembling hands, I would race through my words more quickly than when I had practiced. I believe, subconsciously, my intent was to get done and sit down as fast as I could. The moment I was finished and back in my seat where I was safe, an incredible feeling of defeat would come over me. It was during those experiences in my seventh grade speech class when I told myself that was what I wanted to do when I grew up; though fearful of speaking, I decided then that I wanted to stand and speak in front of hundreds of people to share a message that was life changing for those who listened.

I wish I could say I finished school knowing exactly what I wanted to do, that I had my life all planned out and I immediately began the pursuit to follow my dream; however, that wasn't the case. I had a desire, but I didn't have a plan. It has been a long journey to get to this point in my career, and I am still on that journey, figuring out where I am going next along the way. At times I have wished I would have taken a much shorter, more direct route, and then I would realize the path I took is exactly the path that I was to take. All the experiences I have been through - the detours I have taken, the struggles, the heartaches, the joys, and excitement – have all contributed to my success and the person I have become.

As a little girl, when someone would ask me what I wanted to be when I grew up, I had two answers. One was to be a mom; the other was to be a teacher. My father worked at a lumber mill where they would receive outdated textbooks from the schools to be disposed of, and he would often bring some of the textbooks home for my siblings and me to read or play with. I loved when he brought these books home. I would sit my younger siblings down with a textbook, paper, and pencil and pretend I was their teacher. I felt pretty special. At the time, my understanding of being a teacher was to stand in front of a classroom of 20 or so students to lecture them and give them assignments, just as they did when I went to school.

By the time I was in middle school, I had decided being a teacher was not for me. Though I enjoyed teaching others, the idea of going to the same classroom and teaching the same students day in and day out was no longer appealing; I needed more variety so I began to consider other options. Many people told me I should be an engineer because I excelled at math, but engineering was not enticing either. I considered being a lawyer, but I feared the possibility of defending someone who was dishonest or had values not in alignment with my own. I took assessments to determine what career choices were suitable for me based on my strengths. I was a bit dumbfounded when one of the results came back stating I should be a criminal sketch artist (I was not very artistic and though I enjoyed art and I sketched a few things here and there, I was not passionate about it enough to work at building my artistic skills; additionally, the thought of sketching a criminal…not something I was interested in). I dreamed of being a writer – I entered a young authors contest in the fourth grade and received honorable mention. I thought of being a florist because I loved the beauty of flowers. I considered many options as I enjoyed so many different things, but there wasn't anything that I could think of at that moment that I loved enough to make it my lifelong career – after all, that's such a long time to make a commitment and stick to it. I just couldn't figure out what I wanted to do when I grew up.

As I graduated from high school, I settled on the idea of studying psychology and becoming a counselor because of my love for helping people. I had a passion for building up others, helping them gain confidence, and doing what I could to make an impactful difference in their lives (and perhaps even change the world). However, when I got into college and took a psychology class, I found it to be extremely dull. It was filled with teaching about famous psychologist of the past who had some very off the wall philosophies that I just couldn't grasp or believe in. Based on this, I decided psychology – as I understood it - wasn't for me.

I then stumbled across accounting. I didn't know what accounting was; it was merely a class I took to fulfill one of my general requirements – and I loved it! It was full of numbers and it stimulated the analytical part of my brain. However, what occurred to me (and the reason I chose to get a bachelor's degree in accounting) was that with an accounting degree I could open up my own business...starting my own business - that was my new dream.

It was during my second year of college when I decided to pursue an accounting degree; I was newly married and pregnant with my first child. Being a mother was important to me, and I wanted to be able to be home to raise the daughter I was soon to have and also have a career. My vision was that once I finished college I could start an accounting business that I could run out of my home. I saw this as an opportunity to be a stay at home mom and still contribute to the financial needs of my family. It wasn't long before I realized that wasn't going to work very well. By the time I had my second child (in my final year of college), it occurred to me that providing for the emotional needs of my children and running an accounting business were not conducive to each other as there would be consistent interruptions to tend to the needs of my children that would interfere with my ability to effectively manage the needs of my clients.

Back to the drawing board I went...unclear of what was I going to do with my life.

I didn't have a plan beyond finishing college. Getting through college while taking care of two babies was a challenge (I consistently took a full-time course load), especially since I was working as in intern in the auditing field while also struggling through a rocky marriage; my goal at that time was to survive and get through college. Most people would have given up and quit, but I had made a commitment to myself and stayed the course, and I'm forever grateful that I did; nonetheless, the day I graduated was the most accomplished and relieving day of my life at that moment.

Right out of college, I took on a part-time job as an office manager for a small janitorial business. I learned many great skills in the area of financial management and bookkeeping. Soon after I began that job, a friend introduced me to a financial services company that was recruiting independent contractors. I saw this as an opportunity to build my own business, so I quickly jumped on board and went through the necessary training and certifications to obtain licensing for selling life insurance, securities, and home mortgages as I continued to work at my part-time job. Shortly after that, I went through a divorce and was forced, as a single mom, to obtain full-time employment.

I never gave up my dream of having my own business. I remarried and had two more children. A few years later I found myself once again as a single parent; nonetheless, I continued to build my financial services business while working a full-time job and raising my four children. I tried out several other business opportunities along the way, and the one that I stuck with the longest was the financial services business. After several years of building my business, I realized, although I enjoyed what I did it wasn't my true passion. I enjoyed working the numbers and giving my clients a plan for changing their lives, but what I loved most about it was sitting down with them and building relationships. I learned so much from my experiences. Being in business for myself and generating my client leads taught me how to push myself out of my comfort zone. What I loved most about what I learned from being in this type of business was the power of intentional personal development as I was taught the importance of consistently reading self-help books and attending workshops, seminars, and conferences. I became engrossed in growing myself. I loved the feeling of continually learning and growing, and as I worked on improving myself and my skills, I also enjoyed sharing what I learned with others and making a positive impact in their lives. I would joke around with my friends and say, "If only there were a way I could do this and make money doing this...." Little did I realize at that time how possible that was.

Overcoming Roadblocks to Success

After a long, arduous road through various jobs, careers, businesses, destructive relationships and single parenting I finally found what I wanted to do 'when I grew up'. I always had my eyes open in search of finding that one thing that I loved. Anytime I heard of a business opportunity, I listened with curiosity, considering whether or not that could be 'the one' for me. One day, I ran across something on the internet that looked like an online business opportunity. I wanted to find out what it was, so I completed a questionnaire. A few days later I received a call. The woman on the other line told me about a training program to become a life coach. I didn't know what a life coach was. When she explained it to me, I knew instantly that was what I wanted to do! I took action and enrolled before getting off the phone. I was a single mother raising four children and working a full-time job. It would have been easy for me to come up with all kinds of reasons or excuses as to why I shouldn't or couldn't immediately jump on board and enroll in the course. I could have easily decided I was too busy or I couldn't afford it. I could never logically explain how the bills were paid every month; we were living on a prayer, but I knew I had been presented with an opportunity to follow my passion and I was not going to make excuses to say "no" and put my dreams on hold any longer. My income tax refund had just come in, and I had plans for it yet I chose to put those plans aside and enroll in the training course, financing the remainder of the cost beyond what the tax return covered.

Lack of sufficient money is a common roadblock keeping people from achieving success. I too had kept from doing many things I wanted to do over the years because of my financial situation. Just a few years before I began my training to be a coach, I had looked into a consulting program through Franklin-Covey. The cost was far outside of my budget, so I made the decision not to pursue the opportunity. I put the idea aside with the purpose that "one day" I would look into it again – when I could afford it. I eventually learned the "one day when I could afford it" was never going to come; there was always going to be something else that I needed to use my money for, and there was never going to be enough money for me to follow my passions, so I just began taking action without knowing how it was all going to work out and I put money into various training programs and business-building tools that I "couldn't afford". What was really interesting is that there was still always enough to pay the bills and put food on the table, so I started worrying less about money and more about finding a way to build my business.

Lack of time is another common roadblock that keeps people from moving forward and becoming successful in their dreams. As I have already demonstrated, I was a very busy single mother of four children and my days were filled with the many responsibilities associated with working and raising children on my own. There didn't seem to be a minute in the day which I could spare; however, once I made the decision to take action, I readjusted my schedule and asked for help when needed so that I could finish my training and start my new business as a coach. I was also very resourceful with my time. I woke up very early in the morning and used my lunch breaks at work to study. On occasion, if I grew exhausted, I took naps in my van and got really good at taking fifteen-minute power naps – just enough to give me the energy to make it through the day. I am not stating this is an ideal routine or schedule; it was what worked for me at the time and allowed me to accomplish what I needed to pursue my dream of owning my own business, and I am now reaping the rewards of pushing myself and working hard.

I gained many valuable tools along my journey to figure out what I wanted to do when I grew up that lead to my success today, but I believe my true success began when I was a child. As a child, I loved the idea of teaching because I had a passion for learning, and this passion stayed with me throughout my life and had been a great benefit to me because continual learning is one key to growing and achieving success. Throughout school, I loved mathematics because there was something intriguing about numbers and problem solving. I later learned that I loved psychology because I enjoy learning how the mind works and how people think and react and I also loved to help people see greatness within themselves that they didn't see. I believe people are like diamonds – some have learned to let their brilliance shine, others are waiting to be discovered. In college, I found a love for accounting because I learned many important business management skills that most startup business owners don't have. I more recently realized I find the most excitement in being a coach because I get to combine all of these passions into one career and do something I am compassionate about and love.

I began to find my diamond within at the age of twelve, two years after my parents separated. My mother decided to go back to college. She had begun college before she got married. She wasn't far into her schooling when she got married and quit college to start a family. As a single mother of eight children she decided to change her life and her circumstances and set an example for my siblings and me on the importance of getting a college education, so the nine of us packed up and moved to a new town three hours away from my home as I knew it and the friends I had grown up with. As I mentioned earlier, I was very shy and insecure, so it was very uncomfortable and scary for me to leave all my friends and everyone and everything I was comfortable with.

I started junior high (seventh grade) that year. On the first day of school, I stood outside during the lunch break watching all the other kids delightfully running around and enjoying their friends who they probably hadn't seen all summer. What a miserable moment that was for me as I didn't know any of them. It was at that moment, at the age of twelve, that I realized my misery was my choice; I had the choice to either continue to act shy, keep to myself, and be lonely as I watched the others having fun OR muster up the courage to go and introduce myself to someone new. It was that day that I received an incredible, life changing experience in stepping out of my comfort zone. I consciously decided I was not going to choose loneliness and I took action to fearfully introduce myself to another girl. Through that one girl, I gained many friends, and what that did to my confidence was extraordinary. I was greatly rewarded for doing the uncomfortable. I learned two invaluable lessons that year. The first lesson was that by stepping out of my comfort zone I made more friends; as I made more friends my confidence grew; as my confidence grew so did my circle of friends because people are attracted to confident people. The second lesson I learned was that stepping out of my comfort zone was rewarding. That one experience was the beginning of a lifelong pursuit of finding opportunities to push me beyond what is comfortable. I am not saying that everything now comes easily. There are still many things that I am uncomfortable doing; I just don't let that stop me from creating success. I have learned that success doesn't come when I no longer have fear; success comes when I take action in spite of fear. By taking action, I can get rid of my fears.

Fear is a roadblock that not only stops but also paralyzes many people from being successful. I believe fear is the key reason people don't take action, whether it's fear of not having enough money, fear of being too busy, fear of not knowing how to move forward, fear of failure, fear of success, or any other fear. There are many fears that hinder a person's success, the greatest one being fear of failure because if fear of failure were non-existent in a person then that person would be sure of success and time and money wouldn't be an issue. I believe Einstein when he said, "You don't fail until you stop trying." What many people call failures I call learning opportunities. When things don't work out, that's all it means – simply that it didn't work. It doesn't mean you failed; it just means that it didn't work. With each moment you find something that doesn't work you have another opportunity to look for what does work and as you learn what doesn't work you are one step closer to finding what DOES work.

Everyone faces roadblocks along their path to success. You will never get to a point in your life or your business that you will no longer face roadblocks, but you can learn to overcome them. Most people quit when they hit a roadblock; don't let that be you. You have greatness. You have incredible potential waiting to be found, so go and find it! You have the key to success, so open the door!

Trudging along your path to finding success is not something I recommend you do alone. The quickest way to reaching success is by working with mentors and coaches. Mentors are important because they have walked the path you are walking so they can help guide you through a less bumpy course by sharing with you what they learned did and didn't work. Likewise, coaches are a crucial piece to achieving success because they can look at things with a new perspective, see things you didn't see, and open your mind to new possibilities. A coach will also push you further than you believed you could go and will hold you accountable for following through to completion. Successful sports players use coaches as do successful business men and women. Why wouldn't you?

Whether you are searching for success in your personal life or you are seeking to build or expand a successful business, I will help you through your journey. I am ready to take you and your team to the next level!

http://www.lifeleadersinternational.com/ or
http://www.catherinemwhite.com

CHAPTER 2

Diane Haugen

Executive Director- North Seattle Chamber of Commerce

Create the highest, grandest vision possible for your life, because you become what you believe. ~ Oprah Winfrey

Catherine: I am very delighted to have with me today Diane Haugen. She is with the North Seattle Chamber of Commerce, and she wants to live in a world where people are inclusive, innovative and successful in reaching their goals. Having spent four years as an Executive Director of the Lake City Chamber of Commerce, Diane engineered a partnership between the Lake City and Northgate Chambers to create the North Seattle Chamber of Commerce (NSCC) in 2012 which then resulted in a larger, stronger network of businesses in the Northeast Seattle area. Diane orchestrates ongoing networking functions, publishes the Chamber's Weekly E-newsletter and assists members in building their businesses. She produces the North Seattle's Annual Summer Festival, SalmonFest Seattle, the Lake City Salmon Bake and Holidays at the Center for her local community.

In 2012, NSCC was awarded the management contract to operate Lake City Community Center (LCCC). Diane is responsible for operations and programming at LCCC. She has filled the local gap in activities for seniors with meals, education, and social programming. She began arts education classes for adults in 2016.

Before working with NSCC, Diane spent thirteen years marketing and managing senior care communities in King and Snohomish Counties, and four years as an entrepreneur food manufacturer. When she isn't working with a chamber, you'll find Diane developing recipes and posting her successes on her new Facebook page, *Kitchen Witch of the North*, and she is also currently developing a new online retail shopping site.

Well Diane, you certainly have a very diverse background and great diversity skills and interests. I think that is just incredible.

Diane: Thank you. It's been quite a road.

Catherine: I would imagine so. We're very excited to hear about that road. I am very intrigued by your *Kitchen Witch of the North*. How did you come up with that name?

Diane: My husband and I used to joke about me being the kitchen witch. I used to have a huge garden with vegetables, fruit trees, and herbs. He would call me the kitchen witch because I would, in a sense, use the herbs for health and healing, and he thought that was rather magical and wonderful, so it was a nickname that stuck.

Catherine: Oh, I love it, I love it, and the food that you post on your Facebook page looks delicious!

Diane: Thank you. Cooking is now a hobby, but I'll tell you that my years as the food manufacturer were just delightful. My goal there was to get my recipes on grocery store shelves, and it was quite a journey from developing recipes, securing a commercial kitchen, getting licensed to produce food for the public and then promoting it to higher end grocers. I would do it all again! Seattle is a hotbed for food manufacturing entrepreneurs, it is. You might have heard of Mama Lil's hot peppers; they are sometimes offered in restaurants; they're available online, and that's a Seattle-based organization that started out selling at the farmer's market and now they're a national product. I had hopes that that would happen for me, but in my case you know one of the hurdles was getting into the right stores at the right time and having the capital to do that; that's one of the challenges of small businesses. As it turned out, there were some changes that kind of stopped me in my tracks. However, when I ended up closing that business, which was called Le Commensal Gourmet Foods, which means "eating at the table together," I closed it with a really warm heart because I did achieve my goal. I had my products in better grocery stores, wine shops, gift shops, up and down the Puget Sound area, and I got really good about getting where I got, and I plan to do it again someday; probably with a different product line, but I plan to do it again.

Catherine: Wow, that's wonderful! You obviously keep yourself very busy as you've been involved in many different things including your work there as the Executive Director at the North Seattle Chamber of Commerce. It sounds like you have done a lot to build up that organization. Would you like to share a little with us on how you got involved with working with the chamber?

Diane: Sure. The North Seattle Chamber, of course, is a blended chamber with the Lake City and Northgate Chambers; we created North Seattle because it made sense. It's a situation that is typical in many neighborhood chambers where you need to stretch your reach. The way that I got involved in this started with what feels like one hundred years ago when I was regularly attending a chamber breakfast in another area, and I was amazed to see how people grew businesses successfully through the true relationships they made there. It wasn't just coming and socializing; these were people that knew how to work the room; they knew how to build relationships, and they followed up. I enjoyed watching how the meetings were run and

17

how there was shared limelight; it was very much a group effort to put the breakfast on and everybody had time to be focused on it. So after thirteen years of managing and marketing senior care communities, I was ready for a change. When the position at the North Seattle Chamber came up the timing was perfect for me, the timing was perfect for them, and that was eight years ago. So really it was something that was always in the back of my mind. I always thought it would be fun and it was the perfect time for me to come in because the chamber was really in a place where it was set to grow; it was set to modernize, and it needed somebody that could carry them forward, and I was able to do that.

Catherine: It's very clear that you were able to do that; I would say you are that person for the job for sure. So what do you say attributed to your success and all that you have done for the Chamber?

Diane: Well, I'm a person of vision, and I also am someone that likes to engage other people and engage new ideas. I can have conversations with people not so much to persuade in a sales way but more with the ability to reason and to be the observer. So here we have a situation, let's look from the outside in and see what needs tweaking, what's working, what's not working and let's troubleshoot where we can take it from here. Our little Lake City Chamber had been in place at that time for about sixty-eight years, and it certainly had both feet entrenched in the past, so being able to bring it forward with everything, I mean this is probably hard to believe now, but I mean at that time you were talking paper newsletters. It was antiquated in that way and so being able to bring it forward, modernize it, start educating our members, thinking about who our membership was at that time and bringing a younger group into the chamber has helped move it forward. We see that happen now with Gen Xers, for example, and now Millennials. Our Chamber president is a millennial. His knowledge has been hugely helpful for the chamber, so it's really about being open to new ideas, being open to new generations of people that have information I don't, and finding that we still have an exchange that's useful for both of us. I can teach them something; they can teach me something.

Catherine: Absolutely, those are very important, and having a vision and engaging other people in having those ideas is just being open and you clearly have to have done a lot of that. You clearly have a vision; I can see that. All that you get involved in is incredible.

Diane: Well, and I think that perseverance is also key. You can't stop. When you hit a roadblock, you can't let that stop you. You need to come back, pick yourself up and go on, even if that idea fails. What is a failure? It's an opportunity to take a look, assess and move forward again whether that failure is an idea, whether that failure is a business, whether that failure is a job, or whatever it is, you just pick yourself up, brush yourself off, let go and move forward because really, it doesn't matter where you've been, what matters is where you're going.

Catherine: What a great message to share with our listeners, thank you.

Diane: You're welcome.

Catherine: So, do you have an example that you could share with us as far as a roadblock that you had faced as you are working towards your successes?

Diane: In this position, the roadblock is usually time. There are always more projects to do than I have time for. Because I balance my work between the Chamber of Commerce and a local community center, because we operate it, there's a huge disparity of time, and I'm always working, really working on time management - consistent list making, consistent prioritizing, and not letting interruptions get in my way; I'd say that is the hardest thing. Also, just being very conscious about utilizing the tools that we have now - being able to use conference calls instead of calling a meeting, scheduling telephone calls which are not something that was always necessary; it is necessary now. With traffic and with time it's hard to get people in one room at the same time. I would say that is probably the biggest challenge and the way that I overcome it is an organization, it is. It's about staying on top of it because if you don't, you really can't be effective in business today, and this job as well as most jobs just require that kind of tenacity to keep accurate records on your calendar and follow through with what you're doing so that you can feel the successes of getting the job done, there's nothing like it.

Catherine: Definitely, and those I think are roadblocks that many people are experiencing. I love how you said earlier that you're going to hit those roadblocks, but you can't stop; you have to keep going and persevere, which is obviously something that you have done and you continue to do.

Diane: Yes, it's key. Having a positive attitude is critical, no matter what. Whatever life hands you, whether it's in your work, your business, whatever it is, the only response is "yes" because when we say "no" to what the universe hands us, that's when we create the roadblock ourselves. So if you say "yes" I can take care of this (it's not always easy, but find the silver lining) people will be amazed that you can do it, and it will help you overcome the stress of unexpected things happening to you, in whatever case it is, whatever part of your life. For me, it's about treating people well and making them a priority in my day, making sure that I'm in the right spot whenever I can be, and I'm the right spot no matter where it is. Those are things that make a difference in my day, and it makes a difference for someone else.

Catherine: Absolutely. So in your work with the chamber, you obviously work with a lot of other individuals - a lot of businesses. How would you say that you have gained all this great information that you're sharing with us today? How do you go about passing that on to the people that you're working with so you can help them get past their roadblocks and reach the successes that they're looking for?

Diane: In my weekly newsletters I always have my column, so I address an aspect of the business that opens the conversation. Whether it's about your business plan, whether it's about networking, whether it's about keeping your customers happy and how to know if they're happy, staying on top of technology, answering what is social media and how important is it, or asking the question, "Is it important to you?" I'm always opening the conversation, and I typically do get responses from my column from people saying, "I see you online...I see you on Facebook... or how can I do that with my business?" People reach out to me, and when I have new members that I know may be new in their business, I routinely reach out to them. I'm picking up the phone (that old technology - picking up the phone) and asking, "How are you doing Joe? How are things going in your business? Is there anything I can do for you?" When I see a chamber member, the first thing I'm going to be saying is, "How are things going and what can the Chamber do for you?" and the usually tells me what they need, and it's quite frequent when I can make a connection for them. I can introduce them to someone; I can introduce them to a resource online, or resource that we have. I help people solve problems. That's probably the best way that I can help people overcome their roadblocks. I really help them solve the issue, do a little coaching and make sure that they're not trying to fix something that is not broken, making sure that they're looking at the key issues that might be affecting their business and also simply coaching about how they talk about their business, how they communicate about it. I keep my ears open about what I see online from them or what I hear them saying about their business. I go out on a limb sometimes. Sometimes I offer unsolicited advice, but kind unsolicited advice, about other ways that they could do what they do.

Most people appreciate that. There are always the people who want to stay where they are, and we certainly see that too. We see people who reject social media, where they might still be sending postcards, I don't know if it's hard to see that. There aren't many businesses where snail mail is the most effective way of communicating with customers. People that reject current technology are those who stay behind and they are not actually an active part of the current business community, whereas people that are open to new ideas and are open to technology are finding some of those openings through the chamber through me, and being able to get to know their local business community better than ever. It's about using the tools we have, and so I end up being a place where they can find the tools they need. I'm constantly asking the questions, "How can we help you? What can I do for you?"

Catherine: That's wonderful! You obviously do a lot for a lot of people, and I love the approach you take in helping people get through their struggles and to move forward in their business. You certainly have a lot of tools that you can share with us, and you are certainly a great resource to go to. Thank you for sharing today. I appreciate all the information that you have given us, and I want to thank you. Have a fabulous day and continue with your successes!

Diane: Thanks so much Catherine.

CHAPTER 3

Gene Hamilton

CEO- I Take the Lead networking groups

The difference in winning and losing is most often not quitting.
~ Walt Disney

Catherine: We are very honored today to have yet another special guest with us, Gene Hamilton, who is the CEO of I Take the Lead. Gene has been involved in Toastmasters, which is a part of a non-profit communication development organization, for almost 30 years. As a leader of Toastmasters in Oregon, Gene won numerous awards and developed the skills to succeed in business and life. He has been a Rotarian for 20 years. Rotary is an organization devoted to being of service to humankind and being a part of numerous community betterment projects. In 2000, I Take the Lead was born and is a company devoted to helping people build their business through word of mouth advertising. Gene and his business partner first started I Take the Lead in Oregon and expanded into Washington in 2005 as a franchise company. Gene is responsible for building groups and seeking out franchises. I Take the Lead builds groups in Washington, Oregon, Colorado, and Florida with a total of over one hundred individual groups. Gene and his business partner feel that I Take the Lead is a kinder, gentler leads group organization designed to help businesses grow.

Welcome Gene, thank you for joining us tonight.

Gene: Thank you.

Catherine: Tell us about your organization, I Take the Lead.

Gene: We started out of necessity because I was an insurance agent. I needed a leads group and there were a million insurance agents out there and not very many leads groups, so it was necessary because I couldn't go to anybody else and join, so I had to start my own. That's how I came to creating it a little bit differently than other leads groups, a little more user-friendly. So, that's what we did.

Catherine: How did you go about starting this group?

Gene: Just one group at a time. We built Portland to over fifty groups; we have groups in Oregon, Washington, Colorado and Florida right now, and we're hoping to grow beyond that as a franchise.

Catherine: Are you still in the insurance business or are you doing this as a full-time career?

Gene: I got out of insurance because I had an opportunity. A friend of mine wanted to buy my insurance agency. He was looking for a storefront and a local business. I could have continued to do it, but it was difficult to run two things at once, so I sold my business, and it gave me the seed money to start I Take the Lead. It just seemed natural to be able to go ahead and sell it and get out and do this full time.

Catherine: When you say that I Take the Lead is a kinder, gentler leads group organization, what do you mean by that?

Gene: Good question. Most leads groups are pretty regimented. They're pretty harsh in nature; they're very laser in, you have 30 seconds to do your commercial and 30 seconds to do this or that and when you're time is up you're done talking and then it's, "Okay you're done." With I Take the Lead I think we're a little more user-friendly and we're a little more conversational. We're modeled after Toastmasters where we're inclusive as opposed to exclusive. Instead of saying, "Well we don't want people," we do want people; we want to build a support network. That's the great thing about Toastmasters - it's like a man underneath you, if you fall off the highwire, we're there to catch you, and we're also there to support each other, to be a mastermind, and to be a support network for each other. I like it because to me it's...I like it because it's a kinder, gentler organization. I like it; not everybody does, and that's okay, but a lot of people do like that, that's what attracts them to our organization.

Catherine: Sure, like you said, some may like it some may not. That's why there are different types of groups out there and different ways in which they are run, right?

Gene: Exactly.

Catherine: What are you most passionate about in your role as the CEO of I Take the Lead?

Gene: Being able to be of service to people, being able to help people. Having that empathy for people coming from Toastmasters where I was scared to death to speak in front of a group and network with people has helped me overcome that fear and I think that's what we do here at I Take the Lead. We help people overcome that fear and better themselves, so I think when you do that you really can't go wrong because you're able to help people.

Catherine: That is very important, especially in this type of organization. You started this in 2000, so 16 years ago, and you've grown quite a bit. You're now in four different states with over 100 individual groups. That sounds like quite a success.

Gene: Thank you.

Catherine: What would you attribute your success to? What do you think helped you get to where you're at?

Gene: First of all, I think it's perseverance. You have to keep going. There's always going to be things happening that are unfortunate and unforeseen, so that's a big deal. I think the biggest thing has the systems in place and I think my partner has done a really good job with putting the systems in place so that you can rely on that and not have to do that all yourself. Get good people involved. Some of those people will do a better job than you do and that's okay because you're bringing their skills to help out. I think that's a big thing - not doing it all yourself. That was a big thing for me. When I started was I was doing a lot of the work. People are happy to let you do all the work, but you've got to back off from that, especially as you get bigger and bigger. You've got to let people fail and give them an opportunity to help. Does that make sense?

Catherine: Yes. You said that you would bring other people in and they may do things better than you do. You said that you're okay with that; apparently, you're not threatened by that. There are a lot of people, especially when it comes to their own business, when someone else comes in who is better at something than they are, many people tend to get defensive. I hear that you do not feel that way at all.

Gene: No, you've got to let people fail, and you've got give people a chance. Some people you think will never succeed and then they do, and others who you think will be great, and they fail. It's hard to tell a lot of times but it's good to give them a chance.

Catherine: What do you think help or makes the difference between those who fail and those who succeed?

Gene: Again, I think it's a couple of things, one is perseverance or persistence because people quit too soon. You know the adage about...I think it was Napoleon Hill who said people quit right before they are successful, within a few steps of where they would be successful, but they quit too soon. The another thing is being able to ask for help and to be coachable because not everybody knows everything. Be able to say, "Okay, I'm making a mistake." I know we have that problem with our franchise. We've been doing this for years. We hope they'll understand that we have a track to run on but they don't always listen to what we tell them, and then they go out and try things that we've already done a hundred times. If they listen to us, they don't have to make that mistake. If they listen to us, then they will be able to avoid that pitfall, that landmine, but if they don't they have to figure it out for themselves. Being coachable I think is huge.

Catherine: What I thought of as you were talking about quitting too soon, and this may be what you were referring to, in Napoleon Hill's "Think and Grow Rich" he tells a story about that the Darbys and their search for gold and how they dug and dug and ended up quitting just three feet from gold. So what you're saying is that you see this a lot in business with the people that you're working with, right? They work at it and then it gets to where it seems too hard and then right before they're ready to take off that is where many people tend to quit.

Gene: Exactly. If they just keep going a little bit further, they would find success. Also, there are people that just don't do the work. There are certain things you have to do, but they're just not willing to do it, and they want to blame everybody else, but it is their fault. It goes back to their coachability.

Catherine: You said that a lot of people just don't want to do the work. What might be some of those things that people tend to turn away from and choose not to do that could help them become more successful?

27

Gene: I think with our leads groups people join, they pay their money and they think it's like an ATM card where you put in your ATM card, and it starts spitting out money; that's not how life works. If you go to work you get paid, and you come home with a paycheck, but as an entrepreneur, if you don't do the things you need to do then you're not going to get paid. If they're not doing the one-on-ones, if they're not getting to know people they could go out of business. People will come into a leads group, and they just expect people to give them leads to getting them money and they say, "Well I'm not going to give you a lead until I get to know you and I can trust you", and so that never happens and then they get upset, and they leave. If they would have done the work, if they would have waited a little bit longer, others would get comfortable with them. If they waited until they found a lead then they would have been successful, but they didn't want to do that, or they quit, and they don't get the reward for that then.

Catherine: What are some things that you do as the leader of I Take the Lead to help coach people along in their business and help them to stay the course?

Gene: We've got a lot of different things. We set up mentors for people; we have people who've been there done that. We have some webinars we set up with some successful people - somebody who has failed who can show this is why they're not failing now because these are the things that they've done. Individual coaching - if they have any questions or maybe it's not working they can always contact us, and we can coach them through it. We offer speed networking events to give them an opportunity to get out and meet people and expand their horizons. We also put on mixers that allow people to get together on kind of a friendship type basis or an informal basis to get to know each other better. We feel like we're building a community that way by getting people mixing and mingling. It's fun and gives them more opportunity to connect. Being in a leads group is one thing but to be able to get out and meet other people that are a great thing.

Catherine: There are a couple of things I heard in that. One was being able to make connections and build stronger connections so that you're not just there to say, "Hello, bye, I want your business, thank you", but you're really taking the time or giving them the opportunity to take the time to really get to know each other and really connect with each other. That makes a big difference in business.

Gene: True, people want to do business with people they know, like and trust; if they don't get to know, like or trust you then it makes it a lot harder.

Catherine: Definitely. Another thing I heard was in providing opportunities for connecting with people who, as you've said, have been there and done that and providing opportunities and stories of people who have been through struggles and have overcome the roadblocks. With that being said, what are some roadblocks that you've had to overcome yourself as you've built this organization?

Gene: I think the key for me has been continuing to build groups by allowing the group members to take over the groups, so we do not extend ourselves out too far. There's too much that it can fail because a group may say, "Oh you're not coming out here and helping us." We want to get them taking ownership and owning the group so that someone else will start another group and not feel like the group will fail. It could still fail, but hopefully, it won't. It's important to continue to expand the organization that way I think.

Catherine: Have you had times when that was very difficult and wasn't where you wanted it to be and maybe times when you felt like giving up?

Gene: Sure, of course, yes, that's always the case. We probably have more dependent people simply because of the nature of our organization where with larger organizations, with larger groups, if they don't have people who have type A personalities who start the groups the group doesn't exist. They have to build their groups, so they're not getting the support that our people are getting. That also creates independence for them so they can build the group. We have smaller groups. We have people who are a little more dependent on us, so it's not a 30 or 40 member group. It's maybe a 4, 5, 6, or 10 member group. It's easier for the group to fail because if a couple of people drop out it's that much smaller; it goes from 8 to 6 or 6 to 4 people. It's a lot different than going from 30 to 25 members, so it's a different dynamic. Does that make sense?

Catherine: Yes, it does make sense. With smaller numbers, you feel that hit or that loss is a lot deeper than you do in a larger group. I also understand that I Take the Lead also has another arm if you will, with a charitable organization, is that correct?

Gene: Correct, yes.

Catherine: Would you tell us a little bit about that?

Gene: Absolutely. We started it several years ago. Rotary does a food drive every year that we support. We call our charitable organization 'Lead With Heart'. We were collecting foods for families in need. We were going to do it at Christmas, but at Christmas and Thanksgiving it seems like there's a lot of things going on, so we moved it to Valentine's Day and that's why we call it 'Lead With Heart.' People also need to eat other times of the year besides Thanksgiving and Christmas, so we did that for a few years then we created a golf tournament. We put together a committee. Next year in August will be our 10th annual golf tournament which will be fun. We do that, and that's our signature because we raise $7,000 to $8,000 a year for local charities which are pretty amazing. We do it on a smaller scale in Seattle and other places. We will pass an envelope around at the groups, and people put a dollar or two or three or ten or twenty...whatever they want to do in the envelope each week, and we use the money to buy food for families in need. Last summer we did it in Washington for about a month, and we raised some money to buy peanut butter for Rotary so they could send the peanut butter home with kids so they would have food during the summer. In Colorado, we did 'Supper with Santa.' It began with one of our members who had adopted his eight-year-old son who was in the foster care system and he found out that he had never experienced Christmas. It was heartbreaking to find an eight-year-old child who had never experienced Christmas. He realized that's common with foster kids, so he created Christmas for those kids. We were able to dovetail that and pass the envelope. It was a simple envelope that went around at all the meetings to collect a little bit of money. Last year we raised over $500 for his program and 100% of the money went to the organization. It felt like it was very expedient in nature and very helpful. I think people appreciated that they could put a dollar or two or five into an envelope and feel like it makes a difference. It's unlike when you drop money in the Salvation Army bucket or watch TV late at night, and they ask for five, ten or fifty dollars and a portion of that money goes toward TV advertising, the CEO's six figure income, and a bunch of other stuff rather than helping the place where it's supposed to go so these people feel like they're getting a bang for their buck really; they feel like it's worthwhile. Contributing five or ten dollars is insignificant; in a lot of places, it's like a drop in the ocean and it doesn't seem to make a difference, but these people feel like these things do, so that's nice.

Catherine: Definitely. I love that you do this as part of I Take the Lead. Being a business owner myself and as a business coach with an emphasis on leadership, I believe in adding value to other people and getting out in the community and making a difference in the community. It is magical because it does something for yourself as well through those that you help. When you do something incredible, something helpful for somebody else it just comes back to you a hundredfold and you feel better about yourselves, so it builds your confidence, and it also helps get your name out into the community so people know who you are and they recognize you and when they need the services that you offer, guess who they are going to go to? They're going to go to the person they, like you said, know, like and trust, right?

Gene: Exactly, right.

Catherine: What a great opportunity. I'm familiar with many different types of leads groups, and that's something that I've not heard of within other leads group.

Gene: I'm not aware of anybody else. I think it's too difficult a lot of times because if you have a leads group organization that has tens of thousands of leads groups it's hard to get something like that organized. We want to keep it simple - that's one of our main philosophies, to keep it simple. Passing an envelope around is simple. Obviously, the golf tournament is a lot more complex because it takes a lot of work and it's a committee effort which is fantastic, but it's nice that it's not difficult to pass an envelope around the group and collect money. That's the cool part about it; it's very easy.

Catherine: Great. It sounds like there are a lot of opportunities that you provide for businesses to get out there, to make connections and to grow their businesses. I think that's wonderful.

Gene: Well, thank you.

Catherine: You are welcome. Is there anything else you would like to share with us before we finish up tonight?

Gene: Again, I think the main thing is to keep going - be persistent and don't quit.

Catherine: Certainly. Thank you, Gene, for all that information and for the wonderful tips that you shared.

Gene: Thank you.

CHAPTER 4

Gene Melius

Owner- Car Guys Northwest

Great things in business are never done by one person.
They're done by a team of people. ~ Steve Jobs

Catherine: Welcome to the show today. We have a special guest with us, Gene Melius. He is the owner of Car Guys Northwest who is an auto wholesale business. He has been in the auto wholesale business for over thirty years but took a break from his business for about eight years when he moved to China, where he taught English to the students of the Guangxi University. During that time he also acted as an agent for Central Washington University where he recruited Chinese students to come to America and study at Central Washington University. Gene recently returned to the United States, this past October, to run his auto wholesale business but he continues to teach English to Chinese students through a curriculum he developed himself which is found at www.abcesl.com.

Gene has been a member of Toastmasters for about thirty years and is currently the Vice President of Membership for the Lake City Chapter. He is grateful for the experience he has gained through Toastmasters because without it; he said he would not have been able to teach at the University in China. He enjoys teaching, and he has a great passion for personal growth. Between his personal experiences and the skills he has learned through Toastmasters, he has gained the ability to grow himself and in turn teach and help others to grow.

Catherine: Gene, so you've been in the auto wholesale business for about thirty years; what exactly is an auto wholesale business?

Gene: Good morning Catherine, thank you. The automotive wholesale business is like a middleman. I will buy a car from a dealer that calls me over the phone. It may be a Ford dealer getting a Mercedes or B.M.W. That's not their product. They're not used to the product, and it's not something they would keep. While someone is trying to trade in their car, the dealer would call me, and I would put a bid on the car, buy it and then I would go pick it up and resell it to a Mercedes or B.M.W. dealer.

Catherine: OK, got it. What makes you good at what you do?

Gene: I'm a pleasant person to the extent personality wise. I feel that some people go out into the world with a smile on their face every day and I feel I'm one of those. When somebody tells me something negative, normally I try to turn it into a positive to share with them a positive feeling, and I think that's important.

Catherine: Sure, certainly. Do you ever get that negative stigma that people tend to have when they hear about auto sales?

Gene: Sure, most people don't understand what I do, and so they say, "Oh, you're a car salesman," but it's a higher tech position. I'm more like the bank. When the dealer does call, they feel confident that if I get the car, I own it and I will pay them, so that's a big deal.

Catherine: How do you create that confidence with them?

Gene: It's actually through networking. When I first started years ago I was a car salesman, and then I was a used car manager for a Volkswagen store, and I saw these wholesalers coming to me to sell me cars, and I thought their job was unique. Many of them would have boats and planes that they would give me rides on because I didn't have one. Their time was so great as far as flexibility. I thought, "You know what, that's something I could do easily," and because of the schedule in the Northwest, being able to go to the cabin, go skiing, or whatever I wanted to do and still be able to make money with my phone. If a dealer called me, I would put the deal together, and then when I would come back into town, I pick up the car and deliver it.

Catherine: Excellent, and it looks like you've also been involved in Toastmasters for about thirty years; that would be about the same time that you started your wholesale business, is that correct?

Gene: That's correct. A friend of mine who got me into the wholesale business was in Toastmasters. He invited me to come, and I can tell you, it's changed my life.

Catherine: How would you say that it has changed your life?

Gene: Toastmasters is a growth opportunity for someone that would want to enrich their life personally and publicly, being able to communicate with people well.

Catherine: You had mentioned, that without your experience in Toastmasters you would not have been able to do what you did when you went to China and taught the students English. How has Toastmasters made that possible for you?

Gene: That's a great question. I can tell you that, when I was young, I stuttered very badly; so bad that I had to go to speech pathologists in grade school to try to get over my shyness of public speaking and speaking to people in general. By going to Toastmasters, it gave me a self-confidence from my peers that enhanced my speaking abilities.

Catherine: Did you still have that stuttering when you began Toastmasters?

Gene: No, I left it behind. I can tell you, like many other people, if I were to speak to strangers or in a group for any reason, my knees would shake just like anyone else, and I'd be very apprehensive. I guess the greatest thing about Toastmasters is that it gives you self-confidence.

Catherine: Certainly and I can hear that you have come a long way with that.

Gene: Thank you, Catherine, for saying that.

Catherine: You're welcome. Going into how that helped you teach at the university in China, I would like to hear a little bit about your experience of doing that.

Gene: Ok. Sure. I think the best way to teach anyone anything is to try the pick out things of interest that someone else might want to do and share or be able to communicate step by step. I found cooking was the vehicle for me in every class. It didn't matter if it was kindergarten, the university students, or adults we would cook together and that way it was a practical experience and what they learned even in my way of Western cooking, many of the students have never done anything like that before, and they could go home to mom and dad and say, "Hey, I know how to make an omelet," and mom and dad would say, "What's that?". It was a great learning experience for them and me even if it was kindergarten. They loved making - this is funny - fried eggs. They never had peanut butter and jelly before. So many things that they have never experienced, like even a tuna fish sandwiches. These are things that I would change every day so that we could learn new things.

Catherine: I love that. In my business, I work with people to help them achieve great success, and I find that the big successes start with the smaller successes. I think about that as you're talking about teaching these kids something so simple as frying an egg and to them that was huge; that was a success; something that they accomplished that they could be proud of.

Gene: You are right Catherine. I felt the same way, and I thought that step by step by them is achieving something they've never done before, they've never been challenged in that way before, and wow, it was a learning experience for me and them; I grew as much as they did.

Catherine: Absolutely. How do you think that those small things that you created for them - those small successes - how do you think that impacted their learning English?

Gene: Well, I guess the best way to qualify that would be the parents. They would come to me and say, "Hey, your passion for teaching English has affected my child," and I would say, "What do you mean? Please explain." Then they would say, "My child would come home and say, I love Uncle Gene" Wow! Heart touching.

Catherine: Absolutely, I can imagine. I had taken a look at your website a bit, and I noticed you have ABC ESL, and the tagline is "Change your life. The school of your future." I would like to hear a little bit about what that means to you.

Gene: Sure. Like myself, with Toastmasters and even further education, we all sometimes - after we leave school - we don't try to improve ourselves. In my case, I felt that it was necessary, number one with public speaking, but it wasn't just that, it was the confidence. Even in the wholesale business that

I do today. People can have that sincere feeling, that I project, that they feel comfortable. Teaching is the same. The students and the parents have to feel comfortable with you for you to achieve your goal.

Catherine: Definitely. Part of the next tagline on your website says, "Magical way of teaching English and Spanish," and perhaps there's more to the magic than what you've explained but I can definitely hear with what the message that you used in teaching them by finding out what it is that they like, what interests them, teaching them those skills and creating that excitement - I can see that definitely creates magic. Is there anything else that you would like to add to that aspect of having a magical way of teaching?

Gene: Like most students that I came across, especially with teaching English in China, many of them would say, "I don't want to learn English" because it's difficult. We have phraseology and intonations that they don't have in China, and so my number one job was to make it attractive, make it interesting because if it was, then they could grasp it and succeed, step by step and boy that's a learning program for myself as well as anyone else.

Catherine: Sure, and I can tell that you are very passionate about what you do.

Gene: That's correct.

Catherine: I am curious, how did you go from being in the auto wholesale business to getting started into teaching English to Chinese students? That's quite a different arena.

Gene: Well, I thought that I saw the economic collapse come or I thought that I felt it coming and so I sold a couple of houses in Seattle, after going to China three times previously, just to get the feel of it. The first two times I went for thirty days and then the third time I went for six months, and at the end of six months, I rented an apartment over there. I thought in the beginning that I would be doing business because of course that's what I was doing in Seattle. After arriving in China, I soon learned that business would be very difficult to do there. Through my teaching, I was able to open a little café across from a high school in China. That helped me also communicate to the students. The students from the high school would volunteer their time to work in the cafe, and the teachers would tell me that they were the best English students in their class and, wow, that was very heartwarming to hear.

Catherine: I can imagine what a compliment that was to you.

Gene: To them also. They had the work at it, and it forced them to be able to communicate clearly and so it benefited everyone.

Catherine: Certainly. I think you may have touched on this a bit, but perhaps you could expand on this a little more. What would you say makes your program so successful that you can create, I quote, "the best English student."

Gene: I mentioned earlier that not many Chinese students wanted to learn English in the beginning. It's like pulling teeth or dragging them to class, and that's not the student that I wanted. I wanted them to have a passion for it like I do. Once they got into it, the passion developed, and the creativity and the self-confidence that they would gain were just fabulous. We would have Western parties that would involve the parents and so forth at cafes and whatever in the town of Guangxi; that was a great experience.

Catherine: Wonderful. So, not only were you working with the students but you were involving the parents and making this a family learning community; that's incredible.

Gene: Definitely, and not only incredible for them but incredible for me because it was a lovely experience.

Catherine: What makes it incredible for you Gene?

Gene: Just being able to share with families of a different culture. Here I am, not only as a teacher but also as a mentor to the parents, and to them to try to get communication going that they felt comfortable and make them see the achievement and the benefits of what we were trying to do.

Catherine: What kind of a difference do you think that made for the families of these students?

Gene: Oh, they would excel in their class, every student that I had. There's only six in class. There is a school in England that figured out that six was the minimum and the maximum you could teach effectively, so I patterned my school after that. It was an optimal experience as far as some students; they gave me the flexibility and the freedom to be hands on.

Catherine: Now that you are no longer in China and you have created this curriculum that you can continue to teach online, how did you make that transition now that you are not there and live to work with these students where you can be there to cook with them and encourage them? How do you manage your program now?

Gene: The program is managed to the extent that individually I'm able to reach out to them to do something different. How I do it here is I show them, Seattle. We may go to a restaurant, or I may go to a park - it doesn't matter - we would go in a kayak or whatever; you have to understand they've never seen a kayak before let alone experienced it. No that it's not coming to China, it is; they're developing very quickly, but you have to remember, six years ago no one owned a car as far as middle class. Government officials did of course, but the middle class has just blossomed in the last six years and I was able to experience it, see it, and go with the flow and it was amazing. The city of Manji was three million people when I arrived in 2006 for the first time;

when I left in 2015, it was close to seven million.

Catherine: Wow, incredible. I think what you have developed is amazing and how you help people is wonderful and very touching. You've created a way for you to be successful and you've created a way for your students and their families to be successful. What kind of things did you come up against as you went through the process of creating this great program and what kind of roadblocks did you come up against?

Gene: That's a great question. When I first arrived, as I've explained earlier in our conversation, I thought I was going to be doing business, and then after that, I realized that's not going to happen, so I opened my school, before I even started teaching at the University, at a park at a children's museum. I was on the second floor. I had to remodel it and boy that was an experience. I was working through interpreters, and you know the American way versus the Chinese way. There are some differences in culture to getting things done, you can imagine, and that was quite an ordeal, but we got through it. After the school was done, about-about six months into it, the police came to my school and saw my ugly face on the promotional materials, and they asked, "Who is that?" I said of course that I was the manager of the school, and they go, "No, no, no."

I thought, "Well that's lovely." It ended up they called me down to the police station and told me that I would have to close the school. That was my first experience, and it was a little earth shattering because I had spent a lot of money remodeling the school and so forth, but that's when I started teaching at the university and getting my feet wet; I had to come up with a different plan. After four years at the university, I figured it out and had my schools. I had four of them in Nanning. We know now that it was successful but enjoyable. You can succeed in anything if you have a passion for; attitude is everything.

Catherine: Absolutely, that was a pretty big roadblock. How do you think that having that experience has helped you grow?

Gene: That's a great question. As a foreigner in a foreign land, some people say it's communist China which it is, but in reality the Chinese people love Americans, and they love the culture; they love the success of America, and they feel that they want to be part of it so sharing what we can share with them gives us an added cultural experience; it gives us dimension. You have to admit they had it very rough in modern times and nineteen seventy-five, I believe, is when they had their cultural revolution, and they've come a long way.

Catherine: How has it helped you come a long way?

Gene: Well, as I expressed earlier, six years ago they did not have cars. When I first got there ten years ago, everyone was on a bike or electric motorbike and motorcycles, small ones. I was able to see the progress of the middle class in China, and it was a wonderful experience overall. They were growing. I would talk to my university students and say, "Please tell me what you'd like to do in the future," and most of them would say, "I want to take my mom and dad around the world." Today they can do that if they have the means. They just wanted to explore; they wanted to see what else was out there. For me to be able to share with them about Seattle, about Montana where my mother was from, about Portland, Oregon or California...it didn't matter. We would go all around the world today with Internet. Isn't that a great tool for us to teach with?

Catherine: It certainly is. I have got a lot out of speaking with you Gene, and I know that our readers will take a lot from this, especially from your comment when you said a little while ago that you could do anything if you have the passion. What a great message. What a great message that you have shared with the roadblock that you faced in starting this school, putting money into remodeling it then having that taken away from you. Most people would've given up right there, and they would have stopped and just figured that "The dream just must not be for me," "maybe I'm going down the wrong path," or "it's just not meant to be." We tend to come up with all these excuses and reasons and ways to talk ourselves out of our dreams, but you didn't let that stop you; you kept going and you got creative and found another way to make it happen. In doing so, I can see that you have changed the lives of many. That is just beautiful.

Gene: Well Catherine, it's a learning experience for everyone, including me. My eight years in China were some of the best experiences that I've ever had in my life, so lovely. It wasn't just me; it was them sharing their lives; that's important.

Catherine: Absolutely, it takes a team. I hear of people who say they are a self-made success, a self-made millionaire, or whatever - self-made this self-made that - but there is no such thing as self-made because it takes a team. We don't do it alone, and that's really what you're saying. You were part of their team; for those students, you were part of their team, and you helped to guide them so that they could create their success.

Gene: You're right, but you know, it is one of those things that you're explaining about team effort. That team effort helped me grow as a person, and wow, I was blown over by their kindness in the country. I would have originally had hesitation about even going there. My family goes, "Why would you do that?" It was an adventure; it was something that I felt I had to do.

Catherine: I completely get what you said about the growth that it brought for you. That is so true for all of us. I find that to be true myself in my own business. I work with people through coaching and through other programs to help them grow. That's my business - to grow other people; to grow their businesses. In so doing it certainly does come back to me tenfold, maybe even one hundred fold, because I am learning; I am growing as well through that process.

Gene: Of course; it's a beautiful thing.

Catherine: Absolutely. Thank you very much, Gene, it has been a pleasure having you on the show today.

CHAPTER 5

Gina L Guddat

LMHC Psychology

You gain strength, courage, and confidence by every experience in which you stop to look fear in the face. You must do the thing which you think you cannot do.
~Eleanor Roosevelt

Catherine: Welcome to the show, we are excited for another great day with a great guest, and today we have Gina Guddat who is a licensed mental health therapist in Seattle, Washington. She works with individuals, couples, teenagers and families locally as well via Skype and telephone and she loves the diversity of her clients. One of her specialties is working with teenage girls. She spent about fifteen years traveling the country working with them in the area of nutrition, exercise, dating, healthy friendships, and future goals.

Gina also enjoys working with couples on relationship issues. She helps them take a look at their communication style, conflict resolution, and how they can join as a team. When she starts a therapeutic relationship with a client she wants to know where it is that they are going and what their goals are; she is very solution focused. Gina says, "In today's age we don't have five years to do therapy, and so I want to get to the point and give them some tools as quickly as possible and be very positive." Gina takes a holistic approach to overall health. With a strong background in fitness, she combines both physical and emotional health. She believes it's easy to feel overwhelmed by bad habits and negative thinking that interfere with the quality of our lives, but as much as we try, she says our efforts to change self-defeating patterns are sometimes ineffective. Gina has offered humanitarian services in many countries such as India, Africa, Mexico, and Vietnam, just to name a few. She has also been featured in the news on ABC, CBS, NBC and much more. She has earned a leadership award from the President's Council on Fitness in Washington D.C., and she has also been recognized as the Woman of the Year with the National Association of Professional Women.

Welcome Gina, I'm very excited to have you on today. What an incredible background that you have. There's just so much incredible talent that you have, and I'm excited to hear more about what you do and how you got there.

Gina: Well thank you for having me.

Catherine: You're welcome. I also want to add in a little plug for our guests, for those who are reading this. I find it quite ironic with the topic of this book being about overcoming roadblocks that I sometimes find while doing this podcast I run up against several road blocks and today was one of them. We had a heck of a time connecting today with one technical difficulty after another yet Gina you are committed, and the both of us were determined just to get this done, and here we are; we're doing it, and it's happening, and I want to thank you for that.

Gina: Hey, I am flexible especially in Seattle where these storm fronts come in. Sometimes when the rain, the wind and flooding starts in some of our technology go down, so we're being creative and getting this done anyway. I'm thankful to be part of this.

Catherine: Great! To start off, Gina, please tell us a little more about what you do in your line of work.

Gina: Well, as you mentioned I am a licensed mental health therapist. I'm the owner of the private practice, soon to be a group practice, in Seattle and I also have another office close to the airport in South King County in the Kent area. Also, along with that, I've developed a product line that goes along with my mission which is helping couples and women lead a more healthy and happy life. That's the bread and butter of what I do with my practice.

Catherine: How did you end up working in this area?

Gina: Well, I started out when I was eighteen in the fitness industry, and I was one of the first ones actually to become certified before we even had to credential for fitness instructors and personal training. I guess I was on the forefront of that many years ago working in health and fitness, working in gyms, and I started my personal training studio for women. That was something that I could do while I was raising children. Sometimes my clients would bring their children with them to work out. I also held kid's fit classes, and I was working with teenagers as well - the whole gamut! It opened my eyes to the fact that most of what I was hearing from my clients while we were working out were what was going on in their lives regarding relationships. I guess that's really what matters to females is relationships in their life; with their kids, their family, their significant others, partners, and boyfriends. It dawned on me that I could probably use another degree outside of health and fitness and maybe try to go back to school to add a degree in psychology. When I was listening to their lives while we were doing ten more repetitions or two more sets of bicep curls we were also solving some of their days to day problems. As it turns out, I find now that combining the physical health and the emotional health tools has had the best impact on the success of people moving forward in their lives. Every client that comes into my practice now also gets a workout routine.

Catherine: Why do you think that combining those two pieces together - both the physical and emotional health - has been so successful?

Gina: You know, we are complex individuals and just addressing one area of our lives doesn't always translate to helping the rest of it. For instance, we can read and read and stimulate our mind and our intellect but it doesn't always translate to the way we're behaving and the types of things that we're doing in our life to show that we've learned those things. In mental health counseling...we know that physical fitness actually can lift depression and it's one of the best treatment plans for anxiety. I'm not opposed to medicine. I believe in pharmaceuticals, and I know there's a place for them, but begin with having a foundation of fitness. The endorphins, the positive hormones in our body that are produced when we do cardiovascular and strength training exercises give us a better outlook on life. Additionally, exercise can relieve stress by clearing out cortisol. If we can get some of the daily stress out through fitness, then we can better focus on our relationships and the day to day things that we need to focus on without being in a constant worry circle in our mind with thoughts that aren't going anywhere. Physical fitness also goes the other way. As a personal trainer and a group fitness instructor, a lot of times we would have problems with exercise adherence, people not coming into the gym to complete the goals that they said they had for themselves - to become stronger, to become more cardiovascularly fit. In these cases, we do have to get into the psychology of what is preventing these people from actually coming in and doing what they say they want to accomplished in their lives? I've also been fortunate to have worked with some premier athletes - doing personal training and sports psychology to help them get over the hurdle of what's preventing them from their fitness goals. So emotional health and physical fitness work together well, hand in hand.

Catherine: Definitely, I can see that. I've even experienced in my life how those two pieces work hand in hand. I know the days in which I get myself up and out to the gym to get my workout in...it makes a tremendous difference in how my day gets started.

Gina: Oh yeah, I mean, people that work out are more productive during the day, they're more focused, and they sleep better at night. We've known this for quite a while, and so I don't let any session go by with a couple or an individual in therapy without monitoring what they're doing for fitness even if it's just walking, which is great.

Catherine: Definitely, you've got to start somewhere. With all this work that you do with helping people, what area are you most passionate about working in?

Gina: I'd like to say I am a dentist that just does the preventative cleaning. I wish I could have that role, but I'm more like the dentist that does root canals. People come to me when they're in crisis. Honestly I get to be a part of people's major life transitions and that it is a huge honor and that is what I'm most passionate about because whether it's helping a young couple plan their future together, as in premarital counseling, or helping an unhealthy couple part ways amicably (conscious uncoupling is what I've been calling it) the result is positive. I get to see people through grief and loss issues when they've lost a loved one and through birthing babies. There have been plenty of women this year that have been expecting their first babies and what all comes with the stress of that and the changing family dynamic. The most important part of our lives are wrapped up around our relationships, and that's either building them up or breaking them down, starting or stopping relationships, and that is why it's just such a privilege to be part of people's transitions.

Catherine: Absolutely, I can imagine so. That's what I love about what I do in the area of coaching is being a part of those big transitions and seeing people transform their lives.

Gina: Right? Sometimes I'll see all sides. I'll see people getting together, and then many years later I'll see people part ways, or I'll see people through the birth of a child and then the loss of an elderly parent. Having the privilege of walking through those life changes and that journey with a patient is special.

Catherine: So you get to see in many cases just really the whole cycle of someone's life. How rewarding that would be!

Gina: I love it when I have a teenager who's struggling, say in middle school, and they come back to me after they graduate from college to report their success and tell me that it was helpful, whatever I did you know to encourage and support them along the way. I love to see the result as well when people are moving forward towards their dreams and goals.

Catherine: I would imagine how old rewarding that would be. You've clearly created this very successful business and helped many lives with much more that you will be helping in the future. As you've built up this incredible business of yours what would you attribute your success to?

Gina: My answer might be different than a woman that has a different type of business, but with psychology, I would say that my success is based on being able to offer unconditional regard for my patients. They will never be judged by me, and this comes as a huge relief for individuals because they have a safe place to come for an hour to talk about everything on their minds and everything on their heart. Many times I hear, "Oh I've never told anyone this" or "You're the first person who knows this." Of course, everything is confidential and the practice here is under all kinds of ethics codes to be encrypted, etc. so they do know that it's different than just talking to a girl-friend or their neighbor or their sister. Not that everybody gossips, but for the most part when you come in and talk to a stranger in my profession you are hoping, and I guess believing that that person can hold your stories without cringing. So clearing our conscience, releasing any guilt and shame that we hold a big burden off of a person emotionally. I don't know that all counselors can do that because you do hear some incredible things. Just when I think I've heard the most amazing incredible story then tomorrow, there's a different one. I love being able to sit with a person and let them know that they are accepted. As humans, we spend a lot of time trying to make people like us and trying to cover up our faults and our weaknesses in the world, in our workplace, in our family, in our community and it's exhausting. When my patients come in, and they can be transparent and vulnerable in my office, they know I can hold their truth and never judge... that is refreshing.

Catherine: Oh, of course, that would be refreshing for anybody regardless of what your story is - whether it's something extremely personal or maybe not so personal - to be able to open up like that would be just beneficial for anybody.

Gina: It is, and I think everyone needs a therapist. I think it's a healthy part of our team.

Catherine: On the other side of your success I'm sure you've come up against several different roadblocks to getting to where you're at. What are some of the roadblocks that you've faced?

Gina: I don't know if this is a roadblock or maybe just considered a detour or a delay like in our Seattle traffic and sometimes not quite getting to the place we want to when we had thought we would. I had started into my profession fairly late in life, and I raised three beautiful daughters, mostly staying at home. I was involved in the fitness industry, and I had started a nonprofit organization for teen girls. As you mentioned in the introduction, I toured around 50+ cities talking to girls about healthy living, but for the most part, I was an at home mom and doing what so many ladies do try to shuffle three different soccer teams, PTA, dinner, cleaning, and all of that. Because of that, I did not go full time into psychology until they were older teenagers so this put me a bit behind my peers in building my brand and in building this business. It just meant that I've had to work a little bit harder and faster to gain a presence in the market. Now it's funny because several people have told me that I have the label as the female Frazier of Seattle which makes me smile; it's a fun idea.

Catherine: Now looking back at the way that you went about creating your business and delaying it until you were able to raise your daughters, are you glad that you did it that way or do you look back and wish that you would have started sooner? What are your thoughts on that?

Gina: You know, I don't have any regret being home with my kids mostly full time. I think for me it was the right thing to do, but when I talk with young women, I encourage them to finish their college degree at least in a trade or two-year school. There are so many great programs out there now that give you tools where you can support yourself. I delayed getting my bachelor's and master's degree until I was older. Whether a woman decides to stay home with their kids or work flex time, part-time, or full-time in their careers with children, I think if we can get the females to finish their degrees first, that's imperative. Either way...I think if I was to go back, that is where I maybe would have made a change personally. I still would have stayed home with my kids, but I would have gotten my degrees done so that I had that in my back pocket and always had a tool to be able to take care of myself if I needed to.

Catherine: I think that is great advice and I will attest to that. I started my family while I was in college. I got married in my second year, was pregnant with my first child, and I continued with my degree. I was determined I was not going to do like many women do and stop their schooling because their family was starting. I ended up having my first two children while I was in college. It was tough. It was very tough, but I pushed through, and I completed my degree, and it was the most incredible, refreshing and relieving experience on graduation day. I pushed through and got my degree while I was still young, and my family was still new. I'm very grateful for that and I would back you on the importance of getting get your schooling in.

Awesome, that's great. As we get near the end here, I would like to learn about some of your patients and what it is that you see they struggle with the most often.

Gina: My patient's biggest block is always fear. I am presented with all kinds of different things, but my take on most issues is that it's fear because we're creatures of habit and we do prefer the familiar even when it's unhealthy familiar or harmful. You know the phrase we prefer the known evil, so people get used to living their lives restricted by fear, and they're unsure that there might even be a better way. Fear can be rooted in anything, it can show up as anxiety, depression, OCD, phobias, grief, PTSD, panic attacks, you name it. We get stuck, and we can't move forward to fully embrace what the universe has for us because fear is what programs everyone from seeing the different opportunities that might be out there, or experiencing new things such as new people, new relationships, having new adventures, travelling internationally, taking new journeys, trying a new career, or moving out of state. People are gripped with fear about change, making friends, and even trying new foods. My job is to get people unstuck. Once they have that aha moment you see it on their face, and the light bulb goes on. That's my main job with my patients.

Catherine: Helping them get through that fear?

Gina: Identifying it first so that they recognize that maybe it isn't what they think it is - a phobia of an elevator or a fear of going into social arenas. What we're getting right down to is breaking the familiar and doing something outside our comfort zone, and guess what? We're not going to die, or usually we're not going to die. What I say is, "What's the worst thing that can happen?" Then embrace that; walk through it.

Catherine: It's always easier said than done. Just to clarify that, what you're telling us is to think of the worst thing that can happen and embrace that being the worst thing that can happen? So once you've embraced that then what's next? How does that help you get beyond the fear?

Gina: The power that it holds dissipates. When it comes down to this question, the answer...if you follow it all the way as far as you can go is death. For example, if you have a fear of ladybugs. Is that ladybug going to kill you? Is that bridge going to collapse if you go over it? If you get a divorce are you going to be in the food bank line? Are you going to starve to death? If we follow it all the way out, it is fear of death, and that's paralyzing to people. Are you okay with that? None of us know when we're going to die. We have to live today - we have to live fully for today. Embrace all of our opportunities, love all of the people around us and live today.

Catherine: Very well said. Thank you. That was some very great advice; some great tools that you have provided to us today and I'm looking forward to the difference that you can make in so many more lives.

Gina: Thank you so much for having me today.

Catherine: You're welcome.

CHAPTER 6

Molly Harper Haines

Owner- Harper Haines Group

Move out of your comfort zone. You can only grow if you are
willing to feel awkward and uncomfortable when you try something new.
~ Brian Tracy

Catherine: Hello, we are very excited to have Molly with us today. Molly currently lives in Seattle, Washington with her two puppies. She is the founder of the Harper Haines Group which uses an integrated approach to organizational and revenue development built through a lifetime dedicated to innovation and movement building. Recognizing that the whole is affected by the quality of its parts, the Harper Haines Group tailors business models and strategies to focus on a linkage of silos within an organization and to work to unravel inefficiencies and gaps that strangle otherwise successful efforts.

Molly has a very diverse background from fundraising for political campaigns in rural communities to United States Senate campaigns, legislation, and speech writing on Capitol Hill in Washington DC. Molly strives in developing strategies that motivate the disparate groups of people towards specific action while building a base for ongoing support. She also works with a variety of businesses, non-profit and social enterprise organizations, building high-functioning teams and developing revenue and engagement programs from the ground up. Excelling in dispelling fears around fundraising and helping groups develop the skills for quality relationship-based engagement practices, Molly's passion for this work is contagious.

Molly, we can see that you have a very diverse background and we would love to hear more about this.

How did you get started in this industry?

Molly: That's a great question. My uncle was the Speaker of the House in Montana for 28 years, so I think by the time I could open my mouth as a baby I was licking envelopes and stamps for political campaigns, so I was always involved in politics from the get go.

And then regarding my current expertise... one of my main specialties is revenue, either fundraising or investment strategies or finance. Well, I had this one conversation with someone who turned into my mentor, Bob Fitzgerald. And basically, he said, "what is your main goal in life," and I said, "well I want to have the biggest possible impact, I want to help the most people," I was young and excited about those things! And he said, "Well, money is most organization's biggest challenge, the biggest stressor, and if you want to help a cause, help it raise money." And that made such sense to me!

Then, when you put the relationship aspect to it, where if you do this work well, it's a completely powerful exchange, what the person gets who gives money can last a lifetime. I mean, I think getting a sense of contributing to something meaningful is a basic human need. But it's one of the most rewarding things you can do, and whether it's an investment ask for business or a fundraising ask for either politics or non-profits, I find it super fun and very rewarding.

Then, you get to see the impact of what you do unfold because $1 can do so many different things for an agency. So after that conversation, I decided to go into the "dark arts," which is fundraising for politics and then I just didn't say no to any good opportunity. So, I've woven this very bizarre history together which all contributes to me being able to walk into an organization, in crisis or transition or growth and say okay, let's figure out what the problem is and address it holistically. But, it all started in political fundraising.

Catherine: I see, and it's pretty obvious that when you see an opportunity you seize it, and I think that's great. That's very important when you are seeking success. Sometimes we don't know, or we're looking for specific opportunities, but it's good to keep our eyes open to see what opportunities are around us. Sometimes we go in a different direction than we might have intended originally.

Molly: Absolutely. My list of jobs is quite bizarre, but one of my first jobs was working in a dark room in a photography studio. And being in the dark for hours and hours at a time, restoring old photos ... I didn't think I wanted to be a darkroom expert or a photographer or any of that, but the opportunity presented itself, and I was said, "well it's interesting, so let's try it!"

Out of that experience, I now understand how to frame things; it's helped me with the design aspect of what I do, and regarding materials for companies I have a better eye for it because I did that very random job. So it's one of those really interesting things regarding success, if you just say "yes" as much as possible, then it's amazing how your life can weave together.

Catherine: Absolutely...

Molly: And boredom is the worst thing possible in my mind!

Catherine: I agree. In what you said, we can tell that you are certainly very passionate about what you do. You talked a lot about making a difference

59

and having a big impact, and it sounds like you have done that. What would you say contributed to you being successful in creating the impact that you desired?

Molly: That's a great question, and I think the answer is multifaceted. I don't believe anyone is successful in a significant way alone--I think it's impossible. If anybody says that, they are simply arrogant; that's not true!

So, I was lucky that probably three of the smartest people I ever met are my parents and my sister. My parents, Pat and Rusty Harper, actually worked in sexual harassment investigations and management support and consulting. Therefore, as a kid, I think I learned how to use "I" statements before I could read. I would say when you do that it makes me feel this way because...

At the dinner table they would talk about the challenges that their client is facing and the people problems or the staff is unhappy, or this conflict is happening, and what do you think we should do about it? Even when Robin and I were tiny kids. That is such a gift to be able to engage in that level of problem-solving around people problems at such an early age, so I think that is a huge part of it.

Then, as I grew up, I started this business when I was 26 at the peak of the recession. In hindsight, it was probably a ludicrous idea! But, I had colleagues, family, and friends that were 100% behind me and supported me every step of the way. So it's one of these things that I'd like to claim credit for myself, but there's no way this would have been possible if I wouldn't have had folks in such support and who were so smart that they challenged me every step of the way. So I think the key to success is surrounding you with very smart, very capable, compassionate people... that's the key to politics too.

Catherine: Absolutely. Yes, thank you for sharing that. On the flip side, what would you say were your biggest roadblocks?

Molly: You know, I have to say, something I struggled with in politics, to be honest, was my gender and my age, that struggle is real. I experienced a lot of sexism, especially in politics, and only until very recently has my age and my gender been less of an issue. However, I still can walk into a room, and it's filled with older men who are expecting something very particular when they see a young woman walk in.

I often win them over, but it takes me a while. They also have to let me speak and prove them wrong; I don't get the benefit of the doubt. That's not the case for everyone, but it's true for a huge portion of our population.

So it's helpful to understand what your appearance looks like and how that impacts people's perception of you in business. That was especially true for me when I was getting started in the consulting business. When I started, I was in my mid 20's. I had been working in fundraising and organizing for a solid ten years previous to that, but still, it was such a challenge to even get an interview!

That's why, on my website, I don't have a photo of myself. Those were just things I just had to realize and say, "Okay this is a challenge I have to figure out, to figure out how to maneuver this, and I can't let it be a part of my identity. I can't have a victim mentality about it, but I have to understand it." So, at one point after I started the business, my husband joined me in the business and there were times when I said, "Yep, you have to be the one to go do this first meeting because they're not going to listen to a woman as quickly and we need this to be done fast." And that is difficult to stomach, but it's the way a lot of sectors still work, so that was a big challenge for me.

Catherine: So it was a matter of understanding the situation, finding what the roadblocks were, and then finding a way around those. It's clearly not always the way that we like it to be - you have to find what works.

Molly: Exactly, and I think that's probably one of the better skills that I have in being able to read somebody, somebody's motivation. What are they trying to get out of this? I can read a room, that sort of thing, look at someone and see their body language and what their face is doing and what are they are reacting to positively or negatively. I can get a good sense for who they are and how their brain works. And then, what I would do--it's a secret--but I would try to shock them in some way! So, if they are expecting a prim and proper, boring person, I might make them laugh with a slightly ridiculous joke.

Or, if this person doesn't expect me to have financial expertise, I'm going to make sure that I talk about finances, something so that I can change the conversation and change the dynamic a little bit. When people are a little off center, they're open to seeing something in a different way, and so that's one of the things that I probably do the most is figure out how to create a dynamic between people that leaves a possibility open for something different to happen.

That's a challenge, but I think that's a skill more people should cultivate. That's a lot what I help people learn to do. If more of us did this, I think we would have a lot more innovation and creativity in our businesses.

Catherine: That is a skill. So how about as far as the people that you work with, your clients, what kind of roadblocks do you see them coming up against?

Molly: Well, the recession in 2008 was a big issue. And, there are always external factors that are challenging, but a recession like that when everybody freaks out and closes up their pocket books either for investment or for giving, that's a challenge.

But, regarding consistently what I see as a problem is a lack of transparency between a CEO, or ED, and their board and staff. There are a lot of CEOs and EDs that hold control tightly, and communication and information are not flowing freely. That's when a lot of horrible things can happen.

There have been some times when we've been called in because an organization is facing a financial cliff, they don't know what's wrong and believe to a certain extent that they are doing everything right.

Well, I would look at their books and investigate, do some data analysis, have conversations with people and realize that there is a lack of communication and not everybody is on the same page. People might have problems with misaligned expectations, or sometimes you can have a leader that is misleading their staff or their board. So it's that communication piece that is huge.

Another big thing, probably the number one issue I look at regarding vetting a client, is whether they are ready to try something new. Because clearly if what they were already doing is working they wouldn't be calling, or if they are ready to grow they may not know the best way to do it.

Change is very difficult, and when people aren't ready for it, and they do not have everybody on board regarding being ready to change, then the project will fail every time.

Catherine: And how do you help them overcome these roadblocks?

Molly: I think the key is information. Having folks truly understand exactly where they are and the impact of what they have been doing and not been doing. And as soon as I think you're able to paint a very clear picture, connect the dots, say, "this is what's happening with the revenue lines" or "you're having issues with your expenses" or "your communication is off" or "you have a leadership problem"... that's quite common. As soon as everyone gets on the same page about it, it becomes very difficult for any one person to keep in the denial stage and to keep saying, "let's just go harder at what we've been doing already!"

With all the information on the table, it's pretty difficult not to say "okay, well what are we going to do about it; we've got to try something new because this is not working." But that also takes an element of courage so I think the information is huge and doing quality analysis is critical.

I also simply try to support them. It's scary; it's usually terrifying. No one is typically calling me because they are totally happy and nothing's wrong, and they're not worried or nervous about something. So I try just to be with them, listen to them and realize that this is a very personal thing. Whatever challenge they're going through is personal. Pretending that you can separate completely personal from professional is ludicrous. So, understanding their fears, talking them through it and simply caring about them as people goes a long way.

That's what I think is a great recipe for success.

Catherine: What I heard was, the biggest key is listening and by listening you are showing that you care and that you are there and interested in helping them and bettering them.

Molly: Exactly, and asking a lot of questions. Asking about how are they dealing with this personally, how they are feeling about it, what is happening in their gut, do they have tension in their body, etc. That helps us become aware of how we are feeling in a challenging, stressful or exciting time; and with that personal awareness, you can tap into your power as a professional. So, asking a lot of questions about their personal well-being helps build a connection between you and your client, but it also will help them as professionals in harnessing their ability to succeed in times of stress.

Catherine: Wonderful! Well, these were all very great tips that you have given on how we can be and help others better to be successful. Wonderful tips and I appreciate everything that you shared with us, Molly.

Molly: Absolutely, thank you so much for giving me the opportunity to share some thoughts.

CHAPTER 7

Jake Hanes

Owner- Action Tax Services LLC

I am not a product of my circumstances; I am a product of my decisions.
~ Stephen Covey

Catherine: Today I have a guest who is very special to me, Jake Hanes, the owner of a CPA firm in Auburn Washington. Jake leads a team of professionals to successfully operate his practice year round. Have you ever wondered what a CPA does after that busy tax season? Well, for Jake the offseason is spent in the outdoors with his family, conducting public speaking engagements, providing leadership and resources to local boards, and offering ongoing business coaching to his firm's clientele. As a public speaker and a successful entrepreneur, Jake delivers high energy messages that motivate people to take action in life and build highly successful businesses. Jake has been coaching business owners for more than 14 years in every facet of operating and growing their businesses. He has succeeded as well as failed in business, and he shares those experiences, concepts, and tools so his audiences can use to can take a five-year leap into achieving business success. For the majority of his life, Jake battled epilepsy yet amid all the inherent challenges he reached great heights including summiting the five highest peaks in Washington and building several successful businesses.

Catherine M White

Jake and his wife were friends of mine while attending college. We had lost contact for several years until recently when we were reconnected through an unfortunate event. I am very excited to hear about Jake's adventures that brought him to his current success.

Welcome Jake, it's a very good to have you on the show today.

Jake: Thank you very much.

Catherine: How about you tell us a little bit about the journey that you have been on to get you where you're at today?

Jake: I started out when I finished at Central Washington University and did a few years of private accounting work. My entrepreneurial spirit was just bursting at the seams, and I went and started a landscaping company. It was challenging; being a general contractor is very hard, and it went bust.

I went back into the accounting world with my tail between my legs and thought, "I don't know if I ever want to do that again." It wasn't long when I decided I wanted to try again. My wife and I were struggling financially. We weren't doing all that bad but not doing all that good either and we decided to manage an apartment complex. In doing so I was able to do work and bank all that money, and so for three years we paid the price of managing and banking that money, and it gave us the consecrated funds. I say because if it didn't work this time, I would never touch that money again to do something entrepreneurial. We took those funds, and we opened the doors of that tiny little office, and I proceeded to try to make a success as a CPA. It was hard; it was challenging to do it, but I had a great drive to want to grow my business, and I did what I could. We were pretty successful after a few years and then I met a business coach.

There's a great story about him in my book about how I met him and how I reacted to him and all that stuff, but ultimately I joined forces with him, and the rest is pretty much history. He helped me turn my businesses around (I now have several of them) into machines that operate for the most part by themselves without me. I've got staff that knows what to do. They do their work and enjoy their job, and we work as a team, and we love it. Meanwhile, as we speak, I'm looking at another entrepreneurial role to take on; it's going to be fun. So that's a summary.

Catherine: Excellent. You mentioned that you'd got several business ventures that you're in the middle of and you're taking on another one. What type of ventures are you working on right now?

Jake: I just recently, as in today, wrote a check for another CPA firm I'm acquiring this other businesses and that is happening as we speak. We're bringing in this other business to incorporate into our current business and bringing them together to provide excellent services and resources to all of the clients of the other CPA firm just as we do with all of our clients. In the last couple weeks, things have developed, and it looks like I'll be opening a new business for a trampoline park. That's a bigger investment, a different kind of activity. I've been doing lots and lots of research and preparation and all kinds of stuff to make this all come to fruition.

Catherine: How do you decide on what type of businesses you get involved with?

Jake: I once read a book by Action Coach (my coaching company) that gave me a formula on how you determine what kind of risk you're willing to take, what kind of businesses you would get involved in, what are the things that you'll choose to do or what are aspects of the business that will cause you to make a decision as to whether to acquire it or not. I just got a very detailed list so as I search around for business opportunities I see if they fulfill my criteria for purchasing or starting up the business. My criteria include such things as are they a profitable business? How much of my time does it require? What's the capital outlay of the business to get it started? The business of itself how is it running, what do its history and future look like? I look at history as in the tax returns and the future as in what the profit potential looks like. It's a lot of questions in those categories that once I zero in on things that look good I may go and find those businesses that are for sale and see how well they fill those requirements. I also search for other things out there that look like they might work and see how they fit my criterion. Eventually, I'll find some of them, and I'll start a review of the business process and ultimately come down to a decision, but I normally look at a lot of businesses before anything comes to be something I may acquire.

Catherine: Wow! So that's quite a process that you go through in determining what venture you're going to do next; very structured and very planned out, that's wonderful. Now when you think back to your college years, would you have ever imagined yourself being where you're at today?

Jake: Yeah, I've always been an entrepreneur. When I was in college, I did about two or three different businesses. I was a math tutor who is why I'm now a CPA. I made money; it was fun, it was interesting, it was great. In highschool, I ran a great lawn care business that put me through college and other activities for many years of life. I bought and sold that business three times while I was going to college and highschool and all those things. I'd buy and then get started, and I'd sell it and go to college then I'd come back and start up for the summer and then sell it again, so I was just circling through like that as time went on, but I found early on that it was very hard for me to be employed. I didn't survive well as an employee of business. I would go and start working for a company and realize I could make a lot more money doing this on my own or just doing something else on my own rather than counting the hours on the clock as they would go ever so slowly.

Catherine: I can relate to you on that. I've been very much like that myself, but what I've heard in what you said is that the key to your success has been, number one, having a vision (a very large vision at that) and you had started out having this insatiable vision. Then number two was having the drive to keep going no matter what happens. You kept going and you tried many different things, and that's what's gotten you to where you're at.

Jake: Yeah, you know my vision early on was I knew I wanted to be self-employed and then I began to learn, like through John Maxwell's books, what vision was and I developed a complete vision and mission and goals. When I was fifteen years old, I set a hundred lifetime goals, and they gave me a lot of direction and steering where I would go. To date I have completed about, I think it's something like around 64 or 65 of those. Some of them take fifteen years to complete one goal. I'm working on all of them all the time; it's a lot of fun. I've always been a goal setter since early in my highschool years. That has helped me to succeed. Creating a vision has given me the boost that I needed. There have been obstacles that I've overcome in life that has caused me to recognize life's a precious resource and I'm going to make the most of it, and it has truly led me to think of a much bigger picture and have even more fun in recent years.

Catherine: Great. You mentioned obstacles. Speaking of obstacles...you've shared that you battled epilepsy for the majority of your life. How did that play a role in your success or the struggles that you went through to get to where you're at?

Jake: At the time that I had epilepsy I had thousands of seizures. It was not fun. It was hard, but I did not let the seizures determine how I would be and how I would act and what I would achieve. I remember one time when I was fairly newly married, and I had been through a couple of jobs. I had just lost a job, and I was down, and I was staring...I remember the road right where

I was at...I was on the road, and I was in my car, and I was like, "What am I going to do? What am I doing with my life?" I thought to myself, "I'm going to do what one person told me once. I'm going to get myself on social security disability, and I am going just to quit because I could make enough money on social security disability to make ends meet. I could probably even do something more and make a little more money through the government. I went home thinking about that. I contemplated it but it just wasn't in my makeup; it wasn't in my genes; I just couldn't do it; it wasn't right for me. I pressed forward, and I had periods of time in my life where I would have hundreds and hundreds of seizures in a period of few weeks, and it was sometimes nearly debilitating, but then I was cured of epilepsy, and it was a miraculous, powerful experience. My book talks about the way that I went down. It's too long of a story to share tonight, but I will tell you that it was something to behold, the cure of the epilepsy, and at that point I recognized, "Wow, now nothing holds me back, and I will move forward now and reach my vision and my goals and have fun at it." That's what I've been doing the last few years.

Catherine: Wow! That's pretty incredible. You've mentioned your book, a couple of times actually; I would like to hear a little bit more about your book. First of all, what is the title of your book?

Jake: It's 'The 7 Strategies of Highly Successful Business Owners'.

Catherine: Awesome! Very in line with Stephen Covey's 'The Seven Habits of Highly Effective People', which is a great book.

Jake: I love his book. My book talks about his book. I think he's got great principles. My book doesn't talk about any of his stuff; his is personal development, mine is very different in the area of business and how to succeed and be highly successful in business.

Catherine: Wonderful, could you share with us just a few tips? Perhaps some tips that you share in your book? Part of the goal of my project with my book is to provide tools to other people who are on their path, their journey, to be successful in whatever venture that is. What are some of the things you share to help others be successful?

Jake: Well, one of the first things that I discuss in the book comes from my background as a CPA and I discuss how businesses need to structure themselves, and there's a number of things that go with that, but to structure themselves so that they're not paying too high of taxes and so that they're protecting themselves. One of them is to set up an LLC and an S-corporation for their business. I go through that process. I discuss the pros and even the cons of what to do and how to and when to do it, why you do it...that kind of stuff. That's just super important. That's the biggest thing in my own firm as a CPA that I help business owners with is to save tax dollars so I give that as the first and biggest resource and then about 50 other tips for how they can do little things that you can do in your business that will save you a lot of money in taxes. That's part of it. One of the habits is to hire a business coach. I describe the value that I had with my business coach but then also as I worked with this coach forever and ever, I have shared many resources that he has given to me with many of my clients over the years. I also in the book make available all of these resources that you can get that will help you grow your business, like over three hundred ways to market your company. I give the people those excellent resources in the book and it is the way in which when I met my coach, how I turned my business in two years from being just me and a part-time bookkeeper to having eight full-time staff working on their own with everyone doing their job and a machine was created. It became a profitable enterprise that ran itself without me; my business became an investment, and so I share the things that I did with my coach through his knowledge and his dedication to making me do what I needed to do to get to that level over a couple of years. It was a lot of fun. There is lots more in the book. I don't have to give the whole book away, do I?

Catherine: Certainly not. You don't want to do that because you want people to go out buy it. Sounds like a great tool for any business owner to get their hands on or anyone who's looking to become a business owner to get their hands on. As I listened to you, in the beginning, talking about all the different ventures and different businesses that you have acquired, I wondered how in the world do you have time to spend with your family and to enjoy the outdoors? You just answered that question when you said that you've gotten to a point where your business can run without you, and it is now an investment.

Jake: Well, I didn't share this in the book although maybe I should have... there was a point in time where I stayed overnight at my office. It was a tax deadline, and it was just me. I was the guy doing all these people's taxes; they were always counting on me, and I spent the entire night in my office. It was hard. I woke up like four or five times. I was so so so tired, but I had to get this stuff done so I would wake up and do it for a while and then I would try to take a nap then I would wake up again and do it for a while. It was such a hard, hard thing but I was making good money because I was the one guy running the business and I had great clients and things were going pretty okay. Then I met this coach not long after, and the coach was like, "Why are you doing that? What are your goal and objective?" I learned, a little bit the hard way and a little bit the easy way with having a coach about how I could give up a little control and how I could be inspiring and empower to other people by giving them an opportunity to prove who they were and be great staff members as well as great people for my clients to utilize to get things done. I was gradually able to let go of the reins and give the system and procedures and tools to my staff to go for it and serve the clients, and it was fun.

Catherine: Wow, that sounds pretty exciting. It's incredible what you've done - the whole path that you've taken is incredible. Are there any comments that you would like to leave with us today?

Jake: One of the greatest keys to my success is what I do on an everyday basis. If you were right here looking at my desk, you would see that I have a note on my desk right now. I have written down seven things that I will complete today. Those seven things...right now I have five of them checked off for today. My goal has always been on a daily basis to identify the seven things that I'm going to complete that day. It doesn't always happen, of course, but it gives me direction; it gives me focus when I might go off focus for any number of reasons. That alone, goal setting and setting goals like that on an everyday basis has been the key to success for me. That, and surrounding myself with some of the best people...a good business coach, a good attorney, and for all those other people a good CPA - someone who is going to help you out with those things. Surround yourself with someone who will help you maybe in the emotional areas of life - a coach, a personal coach, or whoever that might be. Then balance in life. I have always been balanced in my life physically to be doing things, mentally to continue to learn and educate myself, and emotionally to communicate and have fun and enjoyable things with others and socially that way, and then financially to make the very most of the resources that are so limited to produce the maximum that I can from them. That's been my key to success.

Catherine: That's wonderful. I just have one question about that. You said that each day you do seven things. Is there something magical about the number seven? You have your book 'Seven Strategies...' and then seven things you do daily. Is that just coincidence or was that intentional?

Jake: That's a coincidence. I read that from a book. I always try to read a book every month and that came from an excellent book - Chet Holmes,

'The Ultimate Sales Machine' and I adopted it in full force about seven or eight years ago. It has been the driving thing. Instead of just thinking about goals once a month...I set a lot of goals. I always have five New Year's Resolutions, and I complete five New Year's Resolutions every year and have so far for twenty years. It's always hard to think about those goals throughout the whole year. Once I realized, "Oh, what am I going to do today to work toward those goals?" that was really what turned the tides and has caused powerful success.

Catherine: I love it! Thank you so much, Jake, for being on the show and being a part of this project. Thank you so much for everything you have shared with us today.

Jake: Thank you.

CHAPTER 8

Janel Stoneback

Entrepreneur- Broker with Windermere Real Estate

Some people dream of success while others wake up and work hard at it.
~ Napoleon Hill

Catherine: We're very delighted today for our special guest, Janel Stoneback. What I love about Janel is that she is an example of the concept that many of us have heard of having multiple streams of income. A little about Janel...she is the co-owner of Emerald City Smoothie of Burien and has been for the past sixteen years. She is also a full-time broker with Windermere Real Estate, so you can imagine that she probably keeps very busy. In addition to that, if that doesn't keep her busy enough, she is also an active member of several community organizations. She was the previous president of the Rotary Club of Des Moines and Normandy Park. She has also been a previous president for the Highline Schools Foundation and currently acts as the vice president for the Des Moines Washington Police Foundation. She said that she grew up in the Puget Sound area and has strong ties within these communities. As far as her career goes, she has had some college experience, but mainly she has worked her way into her career choices. Janel thank you very much for being with us today.

Janel: Glad to be here.

Catherine: I would love to start out by hearing a little bit more about you and some of your endeavors that you have been on.

Janel: Regarding my career path?

Catherine: Your career path, your community involvement, etc. Obviously, you are very involved in many different things; you keep very actively. First of all, how did you get involved in these different areas and what brought you to the path that you're on?

Janel: Well, it's funny, I never knew what I was going to do when I grew up. I had a basic education and was always lucky since I was a hard worker that I found really good jobs and opportunities kind of presented themselves and I always jumped on them. Then about 18 years ago I met my fiancé and his dream was to start a business and I wasn't as confident as he was in making that decision but I had the retail background that we needed to get the business going and he had the construction background, so we did our research and decided that we would open a smoothie shop and I still didn't know what all that looked like. I loved building the store, I loved everything about the retail side of it, but I found out quickly that just being in the store day to day was not my niche, so I still had to figure out what I was going to do when I grew up. We decided to expand at a certain point and so I decided that it would be good for our business to get out in the community just outside of our little community borders and so I originally got involved with my first volunteer work with the Little League and I thought it would be a good opportunity to get in front of kids and parents that I wouldn't necessarily get in front of in my personal life and try and get them into our business. It was probably the smartest thing I ever did because there were 400 kids with 800 hundred parents and it was surreal. Our business exploded; our involvement in the community exploded and it just kind of went from there. I decided that that was something I liked and was really good at and so I just got involved with different organizations. Before that, I knew nothing about being involved with your community, and I grew up in kind of a low-income area and probably was more the person that needed help from the community as opposed to being the person that helped the community, so that was a huge turning point in my life. Getting involved with these various organizations gave me the opportunity to make a big difference in my community, and once I figured that out, I just ran with it. I've been doing that now for ten plus years. I can't say enough great things about it and is the part I enjoy most about being a business owner. With those ties, at a certain point, I decided that helping people was something I enjoyed doing. I had already thought about getting my real estate license but never knew really how that fit into my life. I went and got real estate my license and realized again helping people was my passion, and real estate could be a sales job, but that's not how I treat it or how it is in my life. It's very much about being able to help people with a major purchase in their life.

Catherine: Wonderful. Something that I continue to hear as you tell us your story is that you didn't know each step that you were taking. You didn't know where you were going, where you were heading and things were so unclear for you. Most people will look at that unclarity as something that paralyzes them, and they're not able to move forward, or they choose not to move forward, but what I hear from you is despite the unclarity or the unknown you took that step forward and as you did so it started to become clear for you. You took one direction and maybe that wasn't the direction that you felt was the best direction, but you went that direction and then it led you to something else. I hear this pattern of as you move forward you started to find your way and you started to find that clarity. Would you agree with that?

Janel: Oh definitely. I mean, I didn't go to college because I didn't know what I would go to college for. College wasn't something that was big for my family. We didn't talk about it. It wasn't that they were against it, it's just that we weren't a college graduate family. I was always a hard worker, but again, like you said, I didn't know what I wanted to do nor did I have the confidence; that was a huge part of it too. As I got involved with the different organizations and got involved with my own business my confidence level changed and I became less afraid of myself. With real estate, it's funny because I've only been in it for about four years now but people tell me all the time I should have been doing this a long time ago and I did think about it a long time ago, but I was too afraid. I'm used to making everybody else shine. I love building the stores so that my fiancé can run them. I'm a problem solver. I was a research girl; if I didn't have an answer I'd go figure it out, but it was always for somebody else. When it would come time to have that confidence in myself...I would tell people I don't think I could have done it ten years ago. I think I needed these ten years of trial and error to figure out. It's okay to stumble and fall. You've just got to get back up and try again and along the way you find your way and your strength and just focus on what makes you strong. The biggest thing too is I've never been afraid to ask for help. I'm sure every community has it like our community - different resources for small business owners and I remember working with the SBDC (small business development center)which is a local business group in our community and I remember asking the guy "Why doesn't everybody use your service?" He said, "People don't go into business for themselves to be told what to do." That's our biggest enemy of being self-employed is that we don't like to be told what to do. I think that's our worst enemy because we need the help. You get lost in what you're doing and forget that there are other perspectives and other ways of doing things. I've learned not to be afraid to ask, and that's probably been a huge part of being successful.

Catherine: I'm sure. I can hear that. I also hear that as you stepped out and took that first step forward you started to find your path which you didn't know at first. I also heard that you recognized that ten years ago, though you started thinking of becoming a realtor, in a way you were starting the process you had to go through this path...you had to take this journey to get to where you're at. What I often see happen to people is that they get these ideas and when they don't see how to get there, when they don't see how to reach their goals, they just end up giving up and then later look back and become regretful. You kept that little seed in your mind this whole time. You didn't give up that dream, and you didn't let it frustrate you to the point where you were willing to give up, and so you are now able to appreciate the path that you took to get to where you're at.

We've talked about some of the things that you've dealt with and how you got to where you're at, what about some of the challenges of your clients in real estate or your customers in your smoothie business. What kind of people do you deal with on a daily basis and what kind of challenges do you see them facing.

Janel: With the smoothie shop I would say our biggest challenge is employing people. When you start a business, in your mind you see things going a certain way. In over 16 years there have been some generational changes. How we were when we were kids...you hear the story your parents say, "When we were kids...." I swore I'd never be like that, but now I find myself saying, "When we were kids...." That has been the biggest challenge. When we started cell phones weren't even around, and now we're dealing with employee issues with cell phones. We're creating policies for stuff that wasn't even around 16 years ago. This generation needs more instant gratification, and they're very much more entrepreneurial. We're just dealing with a different type of personality than we were dealing with 16 years ago and so we just worked through those challenges.

Our clients ironically have pretty much stayed the same over the years, other than the fact that our business has just grown year after year after year, which we're extremely fortunate and feel blessed for. A lot of that is just consistency. We're now finding that our clients who we were servicing 16 years ago now have their children coming in because the children were always in tow with mom or dad when they came into the shop and now they're young adults, and they are also coming in. We just make sure we provide a consistent product, listen to our people and make ourselves available for our customers and in the community. Everybody knows how to get ahold of us. We just make sure that we run a good business and so that's been successful.

With real estate, the challenges are...it's funny because I've had this conversation lately with a lot of gals. People think you just get a listing and you slap it on the market and the people will come and it's so far beyond that. I'm dealing with people in divorces; I'm dealing with adult children with estates; just trying to guide people that the media hypes things up more than they do. It's a lot more counseling than I ever thought I would be doing and again that's where I found the passion in it because people need help, and it's nice to be able to help people.

Catherine: What are some of the ways in which you help your clients to get beyond the things that they're dealing with. I can imagine when you're dealing with a variety of people in your business with Windermere...as you mentioned people that are dealing with divorce and all these other situations. What kind of things comes into play when you're working with people that make finding a house or selling a house difficult for them?

Janel: We went through some challenges with our shop. We expanded in 2008 when the economy was tanking. We knew before we ever opened our second and third store that we were in trouble because the economy was tanking, but we were so deep into it we had just to keep moving forward. We worked with counselors; we worked with lawyers; it was humbling, but at the same time we survived it and got to meet a lot of really neat people and learn a lot. I always say that's my college education. I don't even like to call it the failure of the store because it was just an experience. Going through that on my own and having been through some really challenging times and having to work with people and going through really stressful situations, I've been able to apply that in just taking a step back and trying to put myself in their shoes as to why they're not getting along or why they are upset or frustrated with the situation and realizing it's probably not me; it's either the emotional or the financial stress. Being able to take that step back and say, "Okay, what are they going through and how can I help?" I then do whatever I can to help within my ability to help. It's all over the board. Every deal is a new challenge. It's just about going to it with no preconceptions and to help wherever I can. A lot of times people just want somebody to listen, and they're not upset with you or anything; it's just a stressful time, and it's hard for some people to manage that stress.

Catherine: With you being there to offer a listening ear to your client, how has that made a difference in their life?

Janel: I work with women that are single that have gone to buy houses, and they thought they would be married and having that experience with someone special; it's just about being their friend.

There are other situations where there's been a death, and the siblings do not see eye to eye. Often it's not about the money; it's the emotions. The house being sold is the final stage in the process, so it's just walking people through it and talking them through it. It's something that most of the time has to be done, and it feels rushed to people at times, and I'm there to help them through the process and help them work through it.

Catherine: Has that helped them? Do you feel that that's helped ease the process for them?

Janel: Oh yeah. I try not to surprise people with stuff. I make sure I'm up-front that people aren't blinded by a situation that might come up. There are very hard conversations sometimes when something's not going right, especially when there's money involved or emotions and high. Each time that I'm able to help somebody through a problem it helps me in the future to be able to know what to do or not to do because I'm going to make mistakes along the way also, but I have to be able to pick up that phone and make those hard phone calls and each time I do it obviously it gets a little bit easier. I just know that by making this career choice, a huge part of what I'm doing is helping people through some tough times in their life. Having gone through it's easy to...you know, everybody likes a story, and my life has created lots of stories. Being able to share my experiences...I know at this point because I have had success and sometimes from the outside looking in it looks like I've got it all together and I'm just this successful business gal and keeping on the business face all the time but you still at this point in my life there are daily challenges. It's important to be able to slow down for a minute, think through those challenges, and determine what can I do differently. If I make mistakes, I take responsibility and take a step back and do things differently the next time.

Catherine: Excellent. That is a wonderful message. I love that you talked about it being a learning process; that you find yourself having a difficult time making those calls but you just do it. You put aside that fear of making mistakes and you recognize that, "Hey I am human and I am going to make mistakes." You just step out and do it anyhow. Again, I've heard this continual pattern that you just take the initiative and step forward, take that first step and do it. Then what you're able to glean from that is that you're learning and any mistakes that you do make you use those as part of your lesson, a very invaluable lesson, as you mentioned. You take the time to step back, slow down and take a look at the mistake and learn from that and learn how you can do it better the next time. That's key to being successful. So many people get caught up in fear of making mistakes and allow that to paralyze them and keep them from moving forward; by being able just to step forward and look at that as a learning process, you're able to make a difference for yourself so you can move forward and start working towards that success. If you hadn't moved forward, you wouldn't have gotten to where you're at today.

Janel: Right. I think balance is a huge part of it too. As a small business, we owners can get wrapped up in our business, whatever it is. If you don't take the time to have the personal time or have...businesses can be challenging, and they can be hard. When we were closing down our store, we were a part of Rotary, which as you know is your community business leaders. It cost me money to be a member of that and while we were going through closing down stores and some financial struggles I had offered to my fiancé that I would leave Rotary to save money. When I had originally got involved with these community organizations, he didn't quite see the value, but by the time we were going through hard times and we had to make a decision of whether to stay a part of this organization or not, we found the value in the organization. Being able to be with people that were outside my personal relationships, my professional relationships, other like minded people that I wouldn't necessarily come across in my day to day life without being involved with these types of organizations and me found it very empowering to be around people that made me feel good about myself and they knew me on a different level than people I worked with or played with. The great thing was most business owners have been through a rough patch and so having been able to share those experiences and know it's okay was empowering.

Catherine: Certainly. Thank you so much for adding that piece. Balance - making sure that you are nurturing not just your business but also your personal life. Another message that I heard from that was that when you're going through these struggles it's very easy and also very common to give up some of the things that have the most value for you because you think that, like you were saying, giving up something that costs such as your membership in the Rotary Club will save you money; however, if you had you given that up you probably would've lost a lot more than the cost of what you're spending by being part of that group. Balance is important in everything - having balance in your personal life and your business life; having balance in how to decide what pieces you're going to incorporate in your business, what organizations you might be involved in, where you're going to spend your money and such. It's not always a cut and dry, black and white answer, right?

Janel: Right.

Catherine: Great. Well, thank you, Janel. You have given us many very wonderful and helpful tips, and I know that the readers will get great value from the information that you have given us. I would just like to close by asking you is there any final thoughts that you would like to share?

Janel: I think people should do what they love. I've watched so many people hate their jobs, hate wherever they are at in their life. I just learned along the way that we all have choices, and we don't have to be victims of our circumstances. Don't be afraid to go out on a limb and certainly don't live unhappily; life is too short.

Catherine: Definitely. That was another great tip. Thank you so much for sharing that with us.

CHAPTER 9

John Chen

Founder- Geoteaming

Champions don't become champions in the ring; they are merely recognized there. ~ John C Maxwell

Catherine: My guest today is John Chen. John is the extreme leader of Geoteaming. He climbs mountains, walks on fire, swims with dolphins in the wild, rides Harleys, and snowboards out of helicopters.

John started Geoteaming nineteen years ago and is a recognized thought leader on digital team building.

He is the Wiley Author of 50 Digital Team Building Games, a top selling business book. John's clients learn how to balance the paradox of competition and collaboration. His work has earned him multiple awards and more than 140,000 clients across the United States and in countries including Spain, France, and Taiwan have experienced breakthrough results. When you meet John, you'll encounter a dynamic, energetic, and effective facilitator who makes friends with everyone. He will help you and your team experience a life changing adventure. John says, "With every big risk comes to a hidden reward. It may not be what you think it is; it may be better."

Catherine: I love that! Things usually aren't what we think they are and often are much better than what I think, but what intrigues me about you, John is your risk taking. You are a great example of being a risk taker, and I would like you to tell us a little bit about your walking on fire.

John: Thank you Catherine, and thank you for the beautiful introduction. So risk taking and walking on fire...I walked on fire about six times and not only have I walked on fire, but I built a fire once. While walking on fire is an incredible experience, building a fire is much harder than walking on it. It's harder because you have to shovel hot coals, the pile of burning hot coals is chest high and about twenty feet wide. The stat is that you lose about five to seven liters of water during that evening when you build a fire. Here's a story if you want to talk about risk taking.

The thing about it is that we did it as part of an Anthony Robbins seminar and there are multiple other places that you can do something like this. What you have to do is prepare yourselves and get yourself into a key state. I've done a little bit of research, and some of the research is trying to say that there's a layer of vapor on your feet that protects you. What protects you is what state you're in. If you're in a state that says I'm going to burn my feet, you usually end up having that happen to you. But if you're in a state that says I absolutely can do this and if you follow the instructions that are given to you, you can do it safely. The first time I did it, it took me over three hours to get prepared for it and the second time that I had to do it, I was helping other people do this and all of a sudden someone turned to me and said, "It's your turn you got to go." So as a helper, we get to walk, but we got to walk after helping over 120 people through the line. I was able to get ready in three minutes, and the two things that I learned from that regarding this risk taking is 1) You hear the lesson of if I can do this what else I can I do? But it's totally a different thing when you do it. 2) It doesn't take forever to get ready or to change. You can do it in just a few minutes if you know how.

That's just a little bit about the fire walking that I've done. The goal is not to walk across fire, but the goal is for each person to get their lesson about crossing that fire. When you celebrate at the end, it's something that you're going to remember forever, and that's where the learning value comes in.

Catherine: Absolutely, I imagine that you would remember that forever. What an incredible lesson.

John: At the end of the night, they celebrate with fireworks. It's like Disneyland.

This seals the learning and experience for 1,400 people who walked from one side to the other.

Catherine: Sure, what a celebration!

John: Yes. What a celebration; that's what life is about to me.

Catherine: Absolutely. Well, we would certainly love to hear more about that. First of all, I would like it if you would tell us a little bit about what you do.

John: My role is the C.E.O. and "Big Kid" of Geoteaming. We specialize in team building that uses technology and adventure. We create a life changing adventure where we use technology and adventure to create some form of human change at the end of the experience. We're always developing some new training program that uses adventure or some action-oriented event with technology. At the end we use that experience to make sure that you learn something at the end of it, does that makes sense?

Catherine: Yes, that's great. How did you get started in this industry?

John: I was a software design engineer, and I have a Bachelor of Science in Computer Science. About seven years into it, I was working at this little software company across the water called Microsoft. I was doing well with it, but I started falling asleep in design meetings. At the same time, I was getting interested in learning and leadership programs. They had this experiential piece inside of it and so during one of these programs I was talking; I was coaching with a group of about 45 people, and there were three people leading that group including a trainer and two coaches. As one of the coaches, I was talking with my trainer, and I said, "You know, I always knew there was something I supposed to do, I just don't know what it is."

There's a lot of people you ask and they say "me too" or "I don't know what I want to do when I grow up," but this trainer said something that no person has ever replied with, "Give me a week and I'll tell you exactly what it is." Well, that was an interesting answer so I had the money and I had the time, so I flew down to Huntington Beach with a coach much like yourself.

Within 48 hours, we wrote the entire business plan for this company which is now known as Geoteaming. What I affectionately call the Jerry Maguire moment, I sent a seven-page summary to 40-50 people saying that this is what I was going to do. For two and a half years, I was doing team building part time, attending conferences and learning how to do this. After two and a half years I was able to leave Microsoft and start doing this full time.

Catherine: Wow, that's quite impressive.

John: Thank you. It's now our nineteenth year, and we've completed over 1,500 events. We do on average about 120 events per year.

Catherine: That's fabulous!

That's quite a business you have going on. You are obviously very successful, and it sounds like you took a rather quick path to that success; that's pretty incredible.

John: I am on the way to the second decade, so I am the best twenty-year overnight success you've ever met.

Catherine: Right. That reminds me of a quote that says something like, "Champions are not created in the ring, that's where they're recognized." That's like what you're saying. For instance, I see a great success that you have now but what I didn't see is all the arduous work and challenges and roadblocks and things that you faced over the years to get to where you are. It's easy, for someone like me, to get caught up in the "well look at how successful you are...wow that was amazing...you're just really lucky" mentality, right? But it wasn't that at all was it? There was a lot more to it.

John: There's a lot more to it. Behind every entrepreneurial success is a story. There are two important things about entrepreneurism. 1) Entrepreneurism is where your dream meets the world's pocketbook. You can have a dream, but if no one's willing to pay for the dream, then it's a hobby. If you want to be an entrepreneur, you need to take that dream and figure out if people are willing to pay for it. 2) Entrepreneurism is how you get over the roadblocks and discover what's working. What you think at the beginning versus what happens is usually different because the market tells you so and your customers tell you so.

Catherine: How did you find that in your business and come to that realization or decision that you had something that people were looking for?

John: That is a good question. The funny part is I built my company backward. I started with the biggest program first. It was twenty-three leaders on a program called The Journey. It was a nine-month training program where six months into the program you attempted to summit Mount Rainier.

This is also another thing for entrepreneurs is to look at your business model. This program is tough because the customer has to be someone who is fit enough to climb, wants to do personal development on the climb and they have the money, time and resources to be on the climb. The good news is we filled all 23 slots as it was the end of the .com era. It was amazing because it totally changed the people on The Journey. It didn't matter if you made the summit of Mt. Rainier or not, it was about YOU getting to YOUR summit. It made miraculous changes to people's lives like people got new jobs, some people moved houses, some people met new significant others in relationships. For one of my clients and very good friends, he applied the lessons when Nokia let him go unexpectedly. Instead of looking at it as a disaster, he immediately rebounded and started a coaching company. He is still coaching people to this date, mainly because of the work that he did during one of our training programs. It was amazing!

Catherine: That certainly is amazing.

John: So, after 2001, the .com thing blew up, and nobody had the money to do The Journey. I was sitting in my office and asked myself, "What am I going to do?" Another key for entrepreneurs is to have an advisor, have mentors, or have other people with more experience in the industry than you do. Make relationships with them and see if they can help you out. I was sitting around not sure what I was going to do next, and my mentor sent me an email. It's one of the most important emails that I have ever received, and it was a sport called geocaching. So Catherine, do you know what geocaching is?

Catherine: I do.

John: Excellent. It's a high-tech treasure hunt with GPS receivers. There are now over two million containers hidden around the world. My mentor forwarded this to me, and he said, "Hey wouldn't this make a great team building event?" He created a GPS-based team building event years before that before the GPS signal got unscrambled. He knew that once the signal got unscrambled it was just going to get better. I contacted the founders of geocaching.com, and they were operating out of their parents' basement at that time. They weren't focusing on events, so they put me on the front page of the website, and I started getting over 100 leads a month. That's when we knew we had something. We did the first team building event with Adobe with about 60-80 people at Discovery Park. You are coaching, and you design training right, Catherine?

Catherine: That is correct.

John: You know when you have something when you have a training program that you can do over and over and over. Sometimes you design a program, and you run it once or twice and then nobody buys it again. Then we created magic with our GPS-based program. From its inception in 2001, people still want to do this - 15 years later and the lessons are just as valuable. We have highly refined it over the last 15 years with over 1,500 events. That's how you know when you have something that people want. What I discovered is that people have a treasure hunting gene, right?

Catherine: Right.

John: No matter what age it is, or wherever, or how old you are people still like a scavenger hunt or treasure hunt. We now run our entire event on an app. So that's how technology is changing, we can design the whole thing, you download it on your phone, it will guide you by GPS to these locations and take photographs and videos and transmit them to a server that we can actually take at the end of it and build a beautiful slideshow and give you all the photographs and videos at the end while tracking your score.

Catherine: Well that's a great story there and great information; it's very impressive how you've been able to carry that on like that and not only carry it on but to adapt it to technology.

John: Thank you.

Catherine: Now as you talk about what you do I can sense a great passion, that you love what you do. I can hear that in your voice. I'd like you to tell me a little bit about what are you most passionate about?

John: So, I am still passionate about three things; First of all, I'm always passionate around the human interactions that we create. Our events create moments and connections between people that they would not normally have, and can also accelerate relationships with people who don't know each other. So, it's interesting. I studied computers for a long time to find out how computers work. Now I get to try and figure out how the human computer works and it is so much more complex than a regular computer, right?

Catherine: Sure.

John: In team building where you put eight people on a team, we have 40-50 different connections between all the different people. Every time you add another person, you get an exponential number of connections with that. That's what's fascinating around team building is that if you add a member to a team or you remove a member to a team, you can change the entire dynamics of that team. I don't think anybody has it down to a science yet. So that's the first thing I'm most passionate around is on the human interactions.

The second thing I'm passionate about is cross team collaboration; this is two or more teams that work together towards a company goal. While being an employee of Microsoft, we had 300-400 engineers who worked on Microsoft

Exchange which was the biggest program that I worked on, and they were divided into five major teams. Those five teams were divided into forty smaller minor teams and getting each of those teams to collaborate one of the ways that I made a success at Microsoft. So I've always been studying cross-team collaboration, and we discovered this law called the law of 80-19-1, have you've ever heard of this law?

Catherine: I have not, that's new to me.

John: OK, it says in a situation where teams are given a team goal and a company goal, 80% of them will just go completely competitive. They'll go for their team, they'll fight with the other teams, they'll try to sabotage the other teams, or just try and beat the other teams. There will be absolutely no collaboration. In 19% of the teams that have the same scenario, they'll attempt to collaborate from the beginning with at least one other team. So maybe they'll strike a deal with one team, or they will try and stop the event and try and get everyone to say, "Hey could we all work together toward this larger goal." They may not succeed, but at least they try. Out of the fifteen hundred or so teams that have done our event, there's only seven, less than one percent who have ever achieved the highest score possible. There's a way for the teams to collaborate at the highest level to take all the revenue or all the points off one of our courses but only seven teams have achieved it. And so, do you know what that tells me?

Catherine: What does that tell you?

John: I'm going to have a job for a long time, Catherine.

Catherine: Great, I love it!

John: Cross team collaboration is a goal that corporate America wants but has no idea how to achieve, and our team building event has shown that. So I think that's really interesting. So yes, human interactions, cross-team collaboration and finally the new one that I'm excited about is gamification. Have you seen gamification growing as a big trend?

Catherine: I cannot say that I have. I'm just not familiar with that so I'm excited to be on this call with you and hear more about it.

John: OK, so gamification in its simplest way is using game mechanics in non-game settings. So again, it's game mechanics in a non-game setting. So for instance, we've been doing conference gamification as we've been running this for the past five years. Let's say you go to a coach's conference but you don't know this app and now we give you all these missions that you can do along the way while you attend the conference so, some of the missions might be you attended a breakout session, or you attended this keynote, what did you learn? Some of them might be conferencing, like meeting three other new coaches with skills in areas you don't have yet, so things like that. A good example is taking a museum; for instance in Seattle we have The Museum of Flight here, and so normally you can walk through the museum and see the Concorde, there's a NASA space shuttle, there are some other things like that; if you're a kid now you may not dig going to these museums anymore but now you can download an app, and we give you points for completing missions that you have to find all over the museum. That's gamification. Does it make sense?

Catherine: Got it, that sounds very fascinating.

John: We're running two programs right now, and we're looking to expand them. We have Boca Raton Resort and then Levi's Stadium. We've collaborated with them, and so we have a game running inside a 1.3 billion dollar NFL stadium. We help them with gamification. We help them turn their playfield into a corporate team building field and so teams now compete and can do things like visiting the Super Bowl was a million dollar suite as missions inside of there while they're competing against other teams. That's what I'm most excited about is that the technology that I have now allows us to create games that our clients can keep going on. So again, if we set this up at the museum for a nominal cost they could potentially have every one of their visitors play this game and so that's something that we're expanding on right now.

Catherine: Wow, you're getting me excited. That sounds like a lot of fun.

John: Imagine you could build a game for all of your clients so they would have to document some of their success during the week. You would get the updates on your phone so you could see how they were applying your coaching through the week.

Catherine: Oh, wow, that's awesome!

John: Anyways, that's gamification at its finest. Other places it's been used is in sales, so people are gamify things like salesforce.com, so if you're a salesperson, you get more points of course for revenue as well as some leads and contacts. Gamification is a super hot trend, and it's growing. There are over 20 million search results on Google, and over eight billion dollars are projected to be spent by 2021. There you go, that's gamification. By the way, I do a breakout on gamification.

Catherine: Well it sounds like you have an incredible product and you are in the right place at the right time.

John: Thank you.

Catherine: Obviously that's not always been the case, right? You've had to build yourself up and get to where you're at to be successful. What would you attribute to your success? I know you mentioned earlier that you worked with advisors and mentors who are more experienced and you are suggesting that to the audience, but is there anything else that you would say that helped you in that success?

John: I have a couple of general ones, and I've got a couple that has really helped me personally. Number one is flexibility. One of my friends has a good quote; he says, "Flexibility is power." Most people don't think that way; they think strong and rigid is power; no, flexibility is power. I think the number one thing that I contribute to 19 years of success...to get to nineteen successful years you have to change. I've changed as the economy, and the environment has changed. We used to have a lot of handheld equipment, in fact, we are just recently cleaned out a lot of our old equipment. We had Pocket PC's as one of the technologies. We had Palm Pilots at one time. These technologies are gone. Like Radioshack or Blockbusters, these things were awesome, and now they're gone. You have to be flexible. We're on an app now. We recognized about three or four years ago an app was super important and so we transitioned to that, and it's changed what we've done. I'd say adding flexibility is the thing that has helped us through any of the challenging times and got us through.

The second one is a no brainer for a team building company - teamwork. I have a large network. We only have about four fulltime people, but we have about twenty different contractors that we use so I rely on the team that I have. I train new team members and getting them to work together is amazing. Just getting the right people together to work together is key and we've done a 2,000 person event, Catherine. We had a core team of 14 who flew in for that and then we also trained over 70 local people for two days before that event before getting it completely right. This was an amazing event. It was in Arizona at Chase Field Stadium and at the end of this event, after they went through an amazing race-like circuit course where they were able to hit in the visitor's batting cage and launch t-shirts at targets we had in the stands, and they built their product logo with each team building a square out of food cans that all got donated to a local charity. At the end of this event, we timed it down to the minute where the last team ran across the line and finished the event, and the roof opened up, and fireworks went off on. Katy Perry's song, "Firework," was playing while the fireworks were going off. There was an immense amount of teamwork that made that moment happen. The number of cell phones that came out and started videotaping at that time told us that we got that right and I have my team to thank for that.

Those are the two general skills. Now I can talk about the three personal skills for me that attribute to my success. The first one is designed skills. When you see a team building event, while it may look fun, I'm telling you everything has a purpose to it. Even if we make you choose a team name and a team shirt or put on a bandana, everything has a purpose to it. I think one of the things that have gotten us through the event is that everything inside of the event is done for a very specific reason.

The second one is facilitation design and presentation skills. As an engineer with a Bachelor of Science degree this is not supposed to be one of my strong suits if I was a typical engineer, but one of I things I learned while I was at Microsoft is that I was one of the few engineers who could also speak and write and that gave me an advantage. That alone in addition to the skill of facilitation and being able to take something that happens during an event and helping to create it as a learning lesson for the group or the individual is one of the biggest skills that I have. In fact, we had an event...so you're talking about roadblocks right?

Catherine: Right.

John: In one of our events we had a key roadblock where a bunch of unexpected things happened. We were near a casino and the casino security, even though I had talked to them beforehand, changed the policy in the middle of my event versus something else we had done before. Things we had done before and were okay had changed, so this event didn't go exactly as I expected. There was one guy in this group who was a dentist, and he got very, very irate with me in the middle of the event. I handled it calm and cool, but the funny part is while he was getting irate he had a coach like you behind him. She was waving her head "No." I didn't see this; she told me the story later that she was waving her head going "nooooo" (like a slow-mo in a movie) trying to tell this guy not to blow up at me. It turns out she had been coaching this guy for over ten years. He had an anger management issue that was going on during this event. Later on in the debrief, as I was on the stage afterward, I asked what people learned. I admitted some of these things didn't go right and I related it to how things sometimes don't go right in your office and I asked what they would do when that happens. This guy raises his hand and says, "John I apologize that I yelled at you during this event." Then he said, " I have this anger management issue, and you know what? I finally used the tool that my coach gave me."

He called it "The Reality Check" and the reality check is, "So what else could this mean?" This was something very simple, and he started doing it, and he asked himself, "Did John design this event to make me mad? No. Does he know me well enough to get me mad? No. I just met him right?"

He talked about all these things and then he said, "John, I'm so excited this event went this way because I now recognize this. I'm going to do this, and I'm making this public commitment that I want to return here in a year." It's a yearly training that they do, and so he said, "I'd like to return in here in a year where not me but my teammates tell me that I'm changed."

That's the power of facilitation. The meaning of facilitation to me is to make it easier and hopefully to make this change easier for this guy. If he's been working ten years on this is an issue, and he changes in a moment and comes back in a year changed, that's a huge, huge piece of value.

Catherine: Oh that is incredible!

John: The last attribute that I have for success is sales skills, something I didn't think I had to learn when I started, but if you're an entrepreneur you're going to have to learn how to sell.

Catherine: Oh darn it! (Laughter)

John: A lot of people will have this exact reaction too. Everyone will go to a lot of the stereotypes like with the used car salesman or anything else like that - all these terrible stereotypes. If you are an entrepreneur, your ability to influence is your ability for your company to be able to survive or thrive. It was so funny, even this weekend I just had a worker garage sale to get rid of some of this extra equipment, and somebody asked me, "Are you in sales?" It doesn't matter what it is, you have to learn those skills, and the skills are showing how your product can help solve their problem and make their life better.

Catherine: Right, and what a lot of people don't understand...like you said, there's a lot of negativity around this idea of being a salesperson, and people tend to want to stay away from that because they don't want to be pushy and they don't want to be known as a salesperson, but in reality aren't we all a salesperson? We all have something to sell whether it's product, a service, or ourselves - like when we're trying to find somebody to date or we're looking for a new job; we are all salespeople. The keyword that you mentioned was an influence; to be a good salesman, is all about the influence that you have on others.

John: The funny part is, I think Catherine when you get it right...what I found for entrepreneurs...this is when you know when you got it right. At the beginning, you're going to have to cold call. You're going to have to call a lot of people who you don't know trying to figure out who's going to get your product. There's a magical point when you get it right, and then it turns around, and your sales become magnetic; that's when people start calling you and saying, "I would like your service" instead of you having to beat down their saying, "Hey, please buy my stuff." That's something you want to look for because once that happens then you know you're definitely on the right track because other people are searching for you and they're calling you and so the energy turns around. For instance, in the last ten plus years, we haven't necessarily had to cold call. We have people coming to our website or meeting us or being referred to us. Over half of our business comes from referrals. There's something magical when you work hard enough in sales that it comes back around and it becomes magnetic; it becomes directed toward you instead of you always having to pull it in.

Catherine: Absolutely. You had to go out and do the work, and now it's paying off.

John: Yeah.

Catherine: There is no easy road, right?

John: No, there isn't. You never know when that's going to stop and something else is going to change too. I've heard of other people's businesses sometimes change overnight because the environment will change; that's where that flexibility comes back in again.

Catherine: Absolutely, great message. The next thing I would like, and you've already mentioned a few things, is for you to go into a little more detail on what the most common roadblocks are that you see in your business that your clients tend to deal with.

John: The number one that I see in our clients is cross team collaboration. Time and time again we will see two to twenty plus teams. I will put you into teams, put a bandanna on you, then have you make up a team name and all of a sudden you react differently to all the other teams in the room. We have a term for it; we call it the reflex. What happens with that...corporate America does this all the time...we put you on a team such as the coaching team or the operations team, and as soon as you are on a team you immediately don't want to work with all the other teams. That is a huge roadblock to our clients - trying to figure out how to get that cross team collaboration and having multiple people work towards a single goal. We see that as one of the most common roadblocks, and it's the greatest piece of value. The funny part is that we're a team building company, but in some in the presence of other teams, you don't have to worry about team building because basically if you put people into three or more teams, they automatically fall into the same behavior, and they go in the competition to either be first or competition to not be last. That team of two to eight people will just bond together trying to do those types of things. You don't have to worry about team building, but you do have to worry about cross-team collaboration. It's very difficult to get people to do this, but we teach this. After watching over 1,500 events, we have a seven step process that we teach as part of the program. That's our biggest piece of value that we're trying to teach as part of our event. So the number one roadblock is cross-team collaboration.

The second roadblock is communication. It doesn't matter if you're a small team if you're just two people or a team of eight, or more importantly five teams of eight. Everybody comes to us with their number one goal as trying to improve their communication. It's usually around making sure everyone is on the same page or the same plan. Quite often what we see is another roadblock called fracture. Let's say you're on a team of eight. If you didn't talk and make a plan and I say go, two of you run ahead, four of you are in the middle, and two are just lagging behind. Nobody's talking with each other, and nobody has a plan about what role they have or what they're doing. Teams commonly make mistakes. We see teams walk one way and then we see them turn around and walk back the other way. They're just wasting energy and effort and so communication and fracture is a very common roadblock that we see with teams. They want to have success in our event as well as with their teams and so I think it gets into that silos piece where people silo themselves into smaller parts. One of the goals they're looking for is creating bridges and sometimes this is as easy as creating a connection with someone on the other team so that they know someone over there. This is what we call to pick up the phone factor. Hopefully, after this event, you feel more comfortable picking up the phone and trying to solve the problem with that person instead of just firing off an email or text or not solving it at all. I think those are the three biggest roadblocks that we see - cross team collaboration, communication and team fracture are probably the three biggest roadblocks to our client's success.

Catherine: How does your organization help them overcome these roadblocks?

John: Number one is an experience. The best part too is, Catherine, I could say you're a bad team member right?

Catherine: Oh well, thank you. (laughter)

John: Yeah, you're most likely not going to listen to me, and you're not going to do anything about that. What happens is that we design these experiences, so the experiences show themselves; they make their determination instead of us telling them where their challenges are. It's what we call learner con-trolled learning. Learner-controlled learning is what we affectionately call 'letting the inmates run the asylum.' What that means is that people can take whatever action...our event only has two goals and five rules. We've seen the game played hundreds and thousands of different ways and what's great about that is that every group can take their experience from that and come to their conclusions. For instance, if you're team is in the last place, that's one of the pieces here is that your experience showed you that the team principles or leadership principles you're trying to attempt to use in a group are not the best, so it gives you a place to experiment with them, to overcome these roadblocks. I think that's the number one most important thing because it's not what I tell you, it's what you learn. It's what you take away from the event that can help you overcome these roadblocks. We've had people come back to us years after later saying, "I still use this lesson today." I still am trying to get people when they get in a multi-team environment, and it's not going well that they will have the skills and tools available to them to say, 'How do I bring this project together?" I tell them they want to learn these tools because it can identify them as a leader inside of the group. When you're amongst five different peers groups, and you can step up into a leadership role, you most likely are going to get pegged for leadership, and you will most likely get advanced for taking that leadership role and taking something that was not successful and making it successful. If you were to take something away from our course, that's what we're looking to give.

Experience is the number one thing, and then number two is tools. We have some tools; one is called 'the seven keys to cross-team collaboration. This is seven steps that have to happen for multiple teams to collaborate and if they don't happen it just falls right back to competition at the end. We do this from our experience of watching all these events; this is a very repeatable pattern. We have something called the 1 CACHE system. It's a six-step system for small teams of two to eight to make decisions faster to make those decisions stick instead of re-making decisions. Have you ever had a client who made a decision and then unmade it and then remade it again later?

Catherine: Oh.

John: Teams do that all the time, and so we have a system to prevent that as well as making sure that the team is completely bought in on the decisions. We use this in a leadership course here in Seattle with the three cohorts and the cohorts used it for nine months into their program including a volunteer project. They said it was invaluable in the fact that they made sure everyone was on the same page before they left their meetings. A couple of other things that we have too. I wrote a book "Fifty Digital Team Building Games" to give resources for people to run their initiatives on their teams to keep team building alive. One thing around team building is it's like software; your team always needs constant upgrades. If you let it just sit and do team building once if you don't keep doing it, then your results are going to dissipate and disappear, or worse, go back into the negative at some point. Even doing small team building events, a little bit along the way, can have huge results. In fact, we have some research that says that if you can actually teach self-facilitation to a group, they can not only keep the gains that they made from a team building event, but they can actually continue and exceed those gains if they just do regular small amounts of team building even if they do it themselves. I also have a five CD out that's called "Top Team Fixes for Team Fails." That's my nineteen years of experience of all sorts of team fails that I've seen. I've described some of them here today but the CDs catalog of all them and talks about an exact fix about what to do with them. That's a whole collection of tools that we give our clients, and of course, I'm trying to make more every year.

Catherine: Well that certainly sounds like a lot of valuable tools that many could benefit from. John, you have given us a lot of great information to-night, and it has been a pleasure speaking with you. Thank you for sharing your successes; thank you for sharing with your clients, how you work with them, and how you help them overcome roadblocks. The one last thing that I want to ask you, and you know we've heard so many great things, but since this is about overcoming the roadblocks of success, I would like to hear a little bit about the roadblocks that you faced as you were building your business and how you overcame those to get to where you are now.

John: Now you're gonna make me think. Hold on a sec....

John: Ok, I got it. So I'm going to talk about two roadblocks that I had to overcome for my success and again, I think if you have a company that will be larger than one, you'll most likely encounter one of these. The number one roadblock for this particular industry is the economy. That's a big roadblock, and it's not one that you can control, so what happens is that team building dies when the economy dies because people stop spending money and it's not viewed as an essential. It's a little bit like marketing. Marketing has the same story too which says that if you have money that you have saved up if you spend on marketing when the economy is down, you will have a huge lead over everyone else. Team building is the same way, but again most people don't think like that. The economy has always been a roadblock to our suc-cess and so just learning how to be savvy around those times to get through them...for us having a contractor, base has really helped us be flexible so that we can expand when the events come and then we can contract instantly if necessary if we slow down. That's one of the key things around the econo-my. You know here's a funny side story too is that team building is a leading indicator of the economy too, did you know that, Catherine?

Catherine: I had not realized that. I didn't think of it that way.

John: So the next time if we have a crash or you want to know when it's starting to come around just call me because what happens is we're a leading indicator of the economy, so obviously no one is buying team building when they're firing people, right?

Catherine: That makes absolute sense.

John: Yeah, but as soon as the firing ends and it stabilizes they start calling for team building for the people who are left. For the last three cycles, I've been able to peg when the recovery has started because my phone started ringing and people start calling saying, "We'd like to do something." Because their team is so battered in some ways for losing people or getting, their budgets cut that they'll start calling. Once they've stabilized that, if they have enough budget for it somewhere, they'll call team building in. That's how we have become a leading indicator of the economy, especially to the economy recovering. That's one of the biggest roadblocks. A second roadblock is, and I talked about it too in our successes, is teamwork and staff. Ironically one of the biggest roadblocks to success in team building is finding the right team-mates to work on team building. Some of them have been great, and some of them haven't been great. I think for any entrepreneur one of your biggest roadblocks will always be finding the best people and then retaining them and figuring out when to keep them and when to let them go. I know every entrepreneur will tell you fire fast but learning how to do that, even for me... after nineteen years I'm still learning how to do that well. I do at least know when it's great. I can say that that's always been one of the biggest road-blocks to success is finding those right team members and then, of course, retaining them - keeping them, especially after you've done training them to get them to a great place.

Catherine: That makes sense.

John: I think the last mention I want to give to overcoming roadblocks to success...those are some of the roadblocks I've got through. One key message is something that you talked about earlier, and that is that passion. You have to have that and I think that's the one thing that will always help you get through all your roadblocks is you having the energy for it and knowing where you're trying to go to. Those are the things. It's much like I told you earlier about the program called The Journey and it's about getting to the summit of the mountain. By having that goal to summit the mountain makes you do all the things you wouldn't normally do. If you're going to go and do entrepreneurship, make sure you understand when it makes you uncomfortable it's making you do something that you didn't think you wanted to do but it's going to make you a better person. If you want the goal, you have to do those things to get it done. I think that's another thing around here for overcoming roadblocks to success is knowing that that's what's happening in that moment. The last part is a lot of your best moments are on the way to success, not at the end - it's not the reward - it's somewhere in the middle. At some moment, and will you have no idea which one it is, you'll recognize it; your emotions will tell you which one it is when it happens.

Catherine: Very nicely put. That was fantastic. I love that! What a great message to end with. That just reminded me of a saying that says, "If you want what you've never had, you must be willing to do what you've never done," and that goes along with what you were talking about with climbing the summit and that journey.

John: Well put Catherine, thank you.

Catherine: Thank you, John. It has been a pleasure to have you on the show. I am very honored. Thank you so much for sharing yourself and your business with us along with your great success stories. We wish you much, much more.

John: You're welcome, thank you so much, Catherine.

CHAPTER 10

Judy Elrod

Business Broker- Murphy Merger and Acquisition Advisors

Instead of giving myself reasons why I can't, I give myself
reasons why I can.
~ Unknown

Catherine: Welcome to the show today. I'm very excited for our special guest, Judy Elrod, with Murphy Merger and Acquisition Advisors. Judy has been a business owner, broker and is a Certified M&A Intermediary. She has over thirty years of experience helping businesses. Judy started her career with Bank of America and rose to become Senior Vice President, heading the regional commercial loan and real estate centers with 150 employees and over a $13 billion dollar loan portfolio. She went on to become a Chief Lending Officer in the credit union industry, and after leaving the financial services industry, she was C.E.O. and founder of a consulting firm focusing on helping businesses from startup to mid-size companies with business strategy and people management solutions. This allowed her to combine her many years of sales lending customer service technology and strategy to service her clients. Judy has handled the sales of over 300 commercial and real estate deals over her career and has been in charge of developing commercial, industrial and retail sites as well. She has owned businesses, so she understands and relates to her client. Judy finds that the future, rather than the past, is the key to stimulating buyer interest and she and the Murphy M&A team work to help clients have a viable, exciting plan in place. Her primary focus is on understanding each client's unique needs and orchestrating the Murphy team of experts to get you where you want to go. She is extremely good at managing the transaction and ensuring her clients get the best deal possible. Judy says selling a middle market business combines both art and science; there's a practical side as well as an art to formulating strategies that maximize your business's perceived value.

Judy, what do you mean by saying that selling in a middle market business combines both art and science?

Judy: I would say it really is an art, it's not a science, but there is a lot of science in it; I mean in numbers, the tax return, the analysis of return, all sorts of information and analysis goes into figuring out the value of the business, and I do that for my clients, that's the science part - the math part if you will. The art is listening to the business owner, understanding everything as much as I possibly can about their business and the unique qualities of that business and then presenting that information to a prospective buyer. Everybody focuses on the numbers, but the real important part is the art of figuring out what is unique about this business and where can it go from here and those type of plans. I like the science, but I love the art part.

Catherine: What do you love most about the art part?

Judy: Getting to know the business owner. I work with small, what I call main street type businesses, up to very large business. Getting to know that business no matter what size it is. Someone, and it's usually the founder, has put in so much work and they have put in so much of their life in order to develop this business, so learning and listening to that story, listening to what their challenges are, perhaps getting ideas and helping to figure out where a new owner can step in and what they can do with this company to take it to the next level. It is like a puzzle; each one is unique. There's canvas to be developed even further, and I get that opportunity to help do that and help show the picture - paint the picture if you will - for a prospective buyer.

Catherine: That's beautiful. I can hear in your voice as you're speaking that you have a real passion for doing that.

Judy: I do, I love it, I love it.

Catherine: Certainly. I know in previous conversations with you; you talked about being able to help your clients realize their dreams.

Judy: Absolutely, exactly. It is what I get to do, and that's the pleasure of it. I serve these business owners and again, listen to their story and what they want to do next to their dream. Their dream may be retirement; their dream may be building another company; their dream may be spending more time with their family; whatever it is, they have a reason for wanting to sell their business. Sometimes it may be health reasons; sometimes it's just "I'm tired." Business owners put a lot of work into their business, and that fatigue can set in and so it's whatever their dream is. I listen to that and find a way for them to sell their business and position their business in a way that I can help them get the most money from it and in turn help the buyer get a business that fits. It has to fit on both sides, so I work hard on that as well.

Catherine: What kind of difference do you think this makes in the lives of your clients?

Judy: Well, I hope it makes a big difference, and I've seen it make a big difference. I've seen people go on to retirement and do the things they want. I see people build a new business as well so it's getting them where they want to go and that's my job - that's what I like to do.

Catherine: Yes. That's very important; it's all about them. Looking at your website, I saw that your company takes the importance of - which you have certainly touched on - the importance of listening and creating those individualized needs rather than using a template or going with that cookie cutter approach and, like you mentioned, not focusing on the numbers so much. You're taking the time to get to know your clients and listening and putting together that individualized and unique program for them and that's critical and very important and I imagine quite meaningful for your clients.

Judy: Absolutely. Each one is different, and that's the pleasure of my job as well; it is why I have a passion for what I do. Each business owner has their unique business, and so it's up to me to figure out...a restaurant is not a restaurant is not a restaurant, for example, so if I am selling a restaurant...yes they have customers and yes they have certain common attributes to other restaurants, but each one is very different, and so I get to figure that out and share that with prospective buyers.

Catherine: I would imagine that not only is that rewarding for them but I would imagine that it is also very rewarding for you.

Judy: That's why I get up every morning.

Catherine: I bet. So, when you got started in this business, clearly you've been down quite an interesting path in the area of financial services and being a business owner and such and you've had quite an impressive portfolio of experience, I'm just wondering, how did you end up in this arena helping business owners realize their dream through the sale and acquisition of their businesses?

Judy: It has been an interesting path. I started out in a management training program for a bank right out of college, so it was my first role. I had good training, but it was just that - training - and then I got to put it into a running.

My first assignment was running a 35 person busy branch office of Bank of America. I walked in, and of course, the people in the branch knew far more than this person that just got off the training program and yet I was their leader. The very first day the power went out; we had to do things by hand, and it was just incredible. I just stepped in and said, "I can do this, I can do this, I can respect all these people and learn from all these people." There were 35 people reporting to me, and I was responsible for our customers so it was a big responsibility but I just stepped in and said, "I can do this, and I can also listen and learn from the people that are already there, and we can work together." I have always taken on positions, and that was a position I'd never been in before, but I figured it out and used my skills. It was also just my energy and working hard to make it a success.

The next place was a 65 person branch; that was incredible. Then I moved into credit, and I had big customers. I had huge customers in real estate. That was the position I got into next with managing a team of lenders. I've been in some leadership positions, and each one I can say was challenging. I had to learn. Continuous learning has been very important and to say, "I can do this," and not get discouraged and not to settle. I keep moving; I keep figuring it out and making adjustments and learning. I guess learning and listening are probably two keys that I can look back and say have made a difference in being successful in my positions and have given me the opportunity to be promoted to another, and another, and another.

Over time that's what I did, and I became Senior Vice President at a very big unit for Bank of America. We went through the process of mergers and mergers and mergers, banks do that, and each time it came with a new challenge, but falling back every time I fell back to that thought, "I can do this", and then I figured out how and I listened to people; that's the way that I did it. Finally, a merger came where they moved my division to Charlotte, North

Carolina. I'm sure Charlotte is the very nice place but coming from Seattle that was not a move I wanted to make, so I left the banking industry and went into the credit union industry as an Executive. That industry was wonderful and fit me well because it's all about serving customers and the needs of its members and so I learned again, after many years. You learn in every position that you get in and every day you learn. You do focus on your members, your clients. The bottom line will come. The bottom line is important, definitely, but put your focus on serving your members, serving your customers. So I thank the credit union industry immensely for reminding me, teaching me, really empathizing that and living it day in and day out. I left the credit union industry also when they became various mergers and went on to work in pulling it all together. I know finance; I've worked with business owners my whole career. I become their mentor. I wear all sorts of hats. I hold everyone's hand through the process. It's a perfect fit for me, I love it, I love it every day.

Catherine: I can tell that you do, and I love that you love it so much.

Judy: It's very rewarding.

Catherine: I imagine. One of the things I heard you say over and over again as you were talking about your experience and your journey is that you kept telling yourself, "I can do this", and you were constantly placed in a new situation where you were inexperienced, and you didn't know what you were doing yet you continued to maintain that mentality and tell yourself, "I can do this", and so you are clearly creating for yourself a belief that you can. How did you get to that place or how did you create that belief when you came across things that you obviously knew that you didn't know how to do and at that moment you couldn't do it. How did you build that belief for yourself?

Judy: Good question; it makes me reflect. I don't know. You can sit and worry and worry is fine because you think things through and you analyze things, but some people come to the conclusion because of the negatives that it can't be done. I've always been a person that looks to all those things and then says, "It can be, or how can it be?" Maybe I can't figure all of the reasons, I'm not the one that is the smart one in many of these departments and units that I ran, but I kept the energy and the focus on how can it be done, what can we do, what do we need in order to get it done? Whether it's a simple thing at home or whether it is a really big deal in trying to figure out how can it can get closed, that's just my attitude. I don't know how I got it; I just don't give up. I truly know that I don't have all the answers and so it's willing to recognize that I have some creativity, but I don't know it all by any means. It's about figuring out the team, who has that answer, who can help me in doing that or to always keep asking that question, moving forward, and making adjustments. Has everything gone right? No, no. I was learning from that. I would say, "Okay, so something went wrong. How do we fix that? How do we make it better? What have we learned from that?"

Catherine: Those are very important questions to ask. How can we, what can we do, what do we need and what can we learn from this? I also appreciate that you mentioned multiple times about going to somebody else and gleaning from their knowledge and their experience and you didn't look at it as, "Well, I'm the leader or, I'm the manager, and I'm in charge of you; therefore, I have to know more than you know." You didn't look at it in that way. It didn't matter what position you were in. You understood that whoever you were managing, they had things that they could teach you and I think that's very important.

Judy: Right, I agree. You can't do it all yourself.

Catherine: Absolutely. You spoke about how you overcame some of your roadblocks. What were some of the roadblocks that you came up against as you went through this journey?

Judy: I think first of all the biggest roadblock is internal. You have to have confidence in yourself or have the 'I can do it' attitude and figure out things. You first start that voice in your head; I guess that's the biggest roadblock. That voice tells you, "You've never done this before Judy what are you doing?" All the things that go on in the head are the biggest ones to overcome so, yourself and the roadblocks that you put up for yourself I think are the biggest.

Then going from there, there are just numerous things that come up. In my time, hopefully, it's changed, when I was in high school nobody encouraged me to go to college, in fact, they discouraged me from going to college because I was a girl; a woman. That was a roadblock that I had to overcome. Frankly, my parents were not supportive of me going to college, so I had to figure out a way to do it by myself and make all the applications and everything. I figured everything out and had gotten it in place by myself before I shared what I was doing with my parents. It was taking those risks. The roadblocks go on and on. For instance, the particular major I was in. You wouldn't believe it at the time, but the business administration and management were my concentration, and there were very few women in those courses. Time and time again, as I walked into classes I was the only one or one of very few women. I had to prove myself time and time again and shine and be the best in whatever it was. At jobs, I would go walking in and run a particular department, and then it became aged, so I was a woman, and I was young and having 40 to 50 people reporting to me. There were numerous roadblocks there and concerns and obstacles that I had to prove myself time and time again.

That's okay. You just keep going, keep going, keep going and keep learning. With everything that I did, every day I learned something. Those are examples of the roadblocks I think that come up. In my business now I'm working with individuals, and they are deciding whether they want to go forward with a sale. I go and work with them; everything is going wonderfully, and then somebody gets cold feet. Even though it's a great fit they have that fear of going forward, so for me it's about helping them to realize, understand, and then answering their concerns. They have their roadblocks, small and big, every day and I just deal with those.

Catherine: Would you say that your experience in choosing to go to college, proving yourself and making it through college is a big part of how you're able to take those experiences into your career in helping your clients through those roadblocks that they face?

Judy: I think that's a good point and yes. Everything you do from when you're young and every day you have things that you learn and you bring with you, and that was certainly one of them for me.

Catherine: I can see how that would make a big difference. That's great, and I love how you have had so much determination and commitment in your life and how you're able to take that into your business to help your clients. Clearly, as you've touched on, they face a lot of roadblocks, and they get discouraged; having somebody like you to be there, to guide them, and to coach them along, I imagine, is what makes the difference in them realizing their dreams like you spoke of earlier.

Judy: It takes all of us working on it, yes. Business owners face lots of challenges. Getting a business started is a challenge but keeping it going is a real challenge day in and day out. I'll do whatever I can do to take something off their plate, take some worry away from them, make it easy for them through the process as they're trying to sell their business, a business that they worked so hard to build; that's my job and my role, to make as easy as possible for them.

Catherine: Yes, and that's very important because starting a business and running a business is quite a challenge.

Judy, I appreciate all the information that you've given; you've given us some excellent points on how to overcome the obstacles that we each face as we go about creating our businesses or even in life in general. Those were some very good points, and I know that those are things that we all can learn from. We can all glean from what you've shared, and we can take that information and use it as an opportunity to realize our dreams. I want to thank you for that, and I want to thank you for all that you do for your clients and for making a difference in their lives.

Judy: Catherine, thank you very much, you're wonderful. I appreciate this time to talk with you.

CHAPTER 11

Lacey Lybecker

Co-Owner- Cairdeas Winery

Take small steps every day, and eventually, you'll get there.
~ Unknown

Catherine: We are very excited for another special guest, Lacey Lybecker, who is the owner of Cairdeas Winery, along with her husband and winemaker, Charlie Lybecker, on the beautiful North Shore of Lake Chelan, Washington. Cairdeas Winery is a true family affair. Lacey, Charlie, and their two boys – Eugene, who is four and Francis, who is two - contribute artwork for Select Artist Series wine labels and are known around the tasting room as the winemaker and assistant winemaker.

Lacey grew up on a farm in Northwestern Minnesota and graduated from the University of Minnesota before moving to Seattle to embark on a career in marketing. She worked in the hospitality and event industry before she and her husband fell for making wine and then moved to the Lake Chelan wine valley area. On the side, Lacey dabbles in designing kitchen textiles with an emphasis on vintage-inspired goods.

Welcome, Lacey. We're very excited to have you today.

Lacey: Very excited to be here.

Catherine: Please share with us how you got into this industry.

Lacey: That is a great question. When people ask, I tell them, "I blame it on my husband's curiosity." I went on my first wine-tasting tour when I was 19 in the Yarra Valley of Australia. I was there traveling for a few months, and it was a fun thing to do on the weekend, and I enjoyed it. When I graduated from college and moved out to Seattle and met my husband, back in the pre-kids day, we'd wake up on a Saturday morning and ask, "What should we do today?" "Let's go wine tasting. Let's go check out the Woodinville Wineries or the South Seattle Artisan Wineries."

It just became something that we did fairly often. My husband was so intrigued by it and everything that went into the winemaking process. If the winemaker were there, he'd be the one talking their ear off and asking a million questions. For the most part, they were all happy to share, which is awesome.

He would ask, "Why is this Syrah so different from that Syrah? Was it the barrel, the vineyard, or the yeast that were used? Was it this or that?" Of course, with winemaking, it's all of those things. I think wine is the perfect industry for my husband because his sense of curiosity is, so to speak, never satisfied. Even for me, the more I learn, the more I realize there is to learn.

We always talked about the big thing that we wanted to do with our lives and winemaking seemed to fit with our vision in terms of what we wanted to do, the "big" thing, so when he asked if we could make a small batch of wine I said, "Yeah, let's go for it." He was just so excited about it. And then he said, "I want to do this again, keep going. And, maybe one day we can start a winery."

I'm a pusher, and my immediate response was, "Why don't we just figure out how to get started now?" We just started digging through piles of information and realized we could convert our garage. We didn't have a ton of money to throw into this, so it was an affordable option. Most people think it's a million dollar minimum to get started in the wine industry, but we were able to get our garage converted into a licensed production facility; we were licensed and bonded, and we scraped up money to buy some used equipment and found somebody who would sell us some grapes to make wine, and we just got started.

It's been amazing because we slowly doubled our production every year and we've been able to build up this business. Sometimes I have to pinch my-self looking back, but we did it one step at a time. We just asked ourselves, "Where are we now and what steps can we take to move forward from here?"

Catherine: That's a fascinating story. What are you most passionate about with what you're doing?

Lacey: Well, obviously, my husband and I love wine and all the intricacies that go into making wine. I'm more of the foodie, so I love the whole idea of pairing food and wine. Both my husband and I worked in desk jobs where you're sitting at your desk, and the most interaction that you have with some-one is a phone call or an email back and forth, so my favorite part and the thing I get most excited about is working in the tasting room and getting to meet so many people from around the area and the state. This region is grow-ing as a wine valley, so we're seeing more people from around the country and the world.

I love connecting with people. Some come while on vacation, and it's a re-laxed environment. I like building relationships and connecting with people over a glass of wine or across the tasting room bar. We get to share our passion and hopefully inspire them to do big things with their lives as well. It sounds kind of funny, but I love that aspect, that one-on-one relationship building with our customers.

Catherine: So this is a great tool for you to, as you said, be able to connect with people and inspire others. I love it! So it's not just about the wine.

Lacey: Yeah, wine is the...it's the glue I guess. We so put so much work and energy into our wine, and it's always the first and foremost in our business. But, the more we put it our wine, the more that we spend time connecting with other people.

I always have a goal or a theme for the year. One of my past themes for the year that has always stuck with me is to "inspire and be inspired." The winery is a great platform for that, to be inspired by other people that we work with either in the industry or the tasting room and then to be able to share what we do and love and pass along that inspiration to others.

Catherine: Before we started the interview I had asked you about the name of your winery. I love the sound of Cairdeas. I had no idea what it meant, but it has a nice sound and flow for this type of business. What does it mean and how did you come up with that name?

Lacey: It's hard to name a winery. Of course, everyone was like, "Why don't you just name it your last name?" We thought that was cool and all but that wasn't really what we wanted. We didn't want just to throw a name out there.

Cairdeas is an Irish Gaelic word that means friendship or goodwill. It is a nod to my husband's Irish heritage and a word that we thought was fitting for a winery. Alliance is another meaning of the word. There is so much camaraderie in the wine industry, so the word alliance is also very fitting. My mom and I went to Ireland, probably 12 years ago. It was right when my husband and I first started dating. It was funny because I didn't know him at that time, but I wanted to take a big trip that year so said to him, "Hey, you want to come to Ireland with me?" He replied, "Yeah that sounds fun." In the meantime, I asked my mom if she wanted to come with me, which was great.

It was amazing. I'm so glad that I got to go on a trip with my mom, but of course, I started dating Charlie, and he was like, "Oh, you're going to Ireland without me, I can't believe it."

While we were there, my mom and I, in this little tiny town, came across this ancient Gaelic written language called Ogham. I guess there are a couple of ways you can say it and it looks almost like hieroglyphics. I'd never seen anything like it, so I bought a few different ones. I bought cairdeas which are friendship, Gra which is love, sonas which are happiness, and I gaire which is laughter. Each was a little character penned on a piece of paper.

These characters were on the wall in our house when we were trying to name the winery, and we kept coming back to Cairdeas and just loved the whole meaning behind it. We took the ancient Gaelic character and worked with a friend of ours who's a graphic designer and he incorporated it into our logo, so it's subtle little nod. The word just gives us the feeling we were trying to achieve with our winery.

Catherine: It is, especially as I listen to you talk about your passion for connecting with people, being an inspiration, and finding inspiration through the work that you do. That name certainly is very fitting for what you do and what you bring to the industry.

Lacey: Yeah.

Catherine: What would you say attributed to your success to as you built up this business?

Lacey: I think a huge part of staying successful for us, or becoming successful, is staying focused on what our vision is and not getting caught up in what other people think. We often hear, "Oh you need to make sweet wine because the market wants sweet wine" or "You should have an event venue because your neighbors have an event venue" or "Where is your Cab Sauv?"

We have a focused niche. We only work with Rhône varietals. That is our niche, our focus. It's about staying true to who we are and what we do in the style of wine that we make.

We always joke that (I read this somewhere) when you're running a race if you turn around and look at the runners behind you and beside you, you're probably going to trip and fall, so it's better to keep your eyes focused forward and run your race. Whenever we get down and out about something, we remember we're running our race. So that's, I think, a big thing.

Another piece of advice that I've heard is, "Focus looks good on you." When we, when my husband and I, are focused on what we're doing, and we're passionate and paying attention to the wine, which is first and foremost, people see that, and people are attracted to that. I think that's a important piece of it.

I come from a marketing background. My husband and I were talking about it yesterday that we could go out and do all the market research we want but if we're not, in this particular business and size of business, if we're not able to do the work and tell a story and be attractive, so to speak, we're not going to be successful. If we just try and put out there what we think people want, how are we setting ourselves apart?

It's important to focus on what we do and do it well. We won't necessarily have something for everyone, but we're going to have everything for someone. We're going to find those people that are interested in what we're doing and connect with that audience.

Catherine: I love how you put that, "We won't have something for everyone but we will have everything for someone." Is that how you said it? That's great. I know that it's difficult in business for a lot of people in making the decision on where their focus is and you said that nicely - don't get caught up in what everybody else wants but instead focus on what it is that these particular people want and provide them with everything that they need.

Lacey: Exactly. I think that's tough, but paying attention to other entrepreneurs, we've learned that along the way that's the most important part. You think you need to branch out, have as many customers as possible, be everything to everyone. It's not about the quantity; it's really about the quality.

We have plenty of people who come into our tasting room that say, "We'd like to your sweet white wines." We tell them, "That's awesome that you know what you love, but that's not our focus. This is what we do. If you're not interested in that, that's totally fine. Let me tell you where you can go to find the wine that you're going to be the most interested in."

We do have people that come in the door, and they're open-minded, or they tell us "Oh my gosh, I love Syrah, and Grenache, and Mourvedre." We then say, "Great! We would love for you to try all of the wines on our tasting flight." The biggest compliment that we get over and over again is, "Wow, I loved everything that I tried." They often say they don't have the same experience at most wineries. Some will say, "Oh, yeah, I like this one" or "I don't like that one" but over and over and over again, people are like "We loved every single wine that we tried." That makes us feel good because we feel like we're doing our job. It's good when other people get excited about what we're doing as well.

Catherine: Certainly, that would be exciting. As you talked about your success, you also mentioned a couple of what I would call roadblocks. Is there anything else, any other roadblocks that you came across as you built your business that brought challenges to creating what you've created?

Lacey: Oh, man. *[Laughter]*

Catherine: Where do you begin?

Lacey: Exactly, where do I begin? Well, I kind of want to throw it out there. On multiple occasions, one of us will get frustrated with something and feel like we're not moving forward. I feel like that's where my husband and I balance each other. When Charlie's down about something, I'll be the one to say, "No, we have to keep going. We're going to get through this. We're going to find some money somewhere." Whatever the issue is, we just have to keep going. We prop each other up in that respect, and I think that's why we make such a good team. We didn't have a million dollars lying around just to throw at a winery. We had to scrape together from our small personal savings. During the first five years of our business, we tucked away a little bit from every paycheck so we could put it towards the winery. We slowly upgraded equipment. As we've increased production we could buy more fruit, maybe we couldn't buy a new press so my husband would be up until three o'clock in the morning pressing wine because we had this tiny press and we would have to do like 15 press loads. We would remind each other, "Don't worry. One day we'll be able to upgrade that equipment." Every year we try and figure out how we can make things a little bit easier and a little bit more efficient on the production side, of course, as we can afford it. It's this kind of challenges and growing pains that you just have to get through and just continue to see that there is light at the end of the tunnel.

Catherine: Absolutely. That is another great example of the work and planning that you put into building a business, and it does pay off in the long run. I know a lot of people hit roadblocks like that and grow very discouraged. A lot of people feel that they can't pursue their dreams because they tell themselves, "Well, I don't have the money to do it. It takes money." You've given such a beautiful example of starting off with just a little bit and working your way up. It doesn't happen overnight.

Lacey: Right. We're in our eighth vintage. We just started our eighth harvest, which is crazy looking back and seeing how far we've come. This year we feel like, "Oh man, we have a business. We're grown-ups, and we have a grown-up business. We need to pay more attention."

I know it is amazing how far you can come if you just put one foot in front of the other. It's crazy, and I tell people this all the time because they say, "Well, I can't do that. We can't do that." I'm like, "Yeah, you can." You literally can start from wherever you are. All you need to do is read, go online and do a little bit of research, or talk to a friend who's in a similar business – anything that you can do just to get your wheels turning and thinking about the future and thinking about what that looks like, then tucking that away at the same time and focusing on one thing at a time. Ask yourself, "What can I do today that's going to get me closer to the next part of this big vision that we have?" I have to pinch myself sometimes because we have this gorgeous piece of property now. We told each other, "Okay, we need a house. We need acreage because we want to plant some vines." This was in our fourth or fifth year of the winery here in Lake Chelan, and we needed a building to do production. That's all we needed. We didn't need anything fancy. We just wanted to get there. Then we found this amazing piece of property with a gorgeous view of the water that was within our budget. This year, we just finished planting vines. We had to build a second barrel house because there wasn't a big enough facility on the property to do production but we live here as well as; our house is on the property, and we have plans to build another larger production facility and tasting room.

We're making it work as we go. I'll sit out on our front patio and look at our little vineyard, and the lake and the mountain…we have a view of the lake (that wasn't even on our wish list), and I look at that, and I think, "Yeah, this is totally what Charlie and I dreamt of eight years ago, and we are here."

Obviously, there is still a lot of work that needs to be done, but this is it. This is pretty amazing. Now we're saying, how can we dream bigger? How can we keep moving forward and dream up something even more incredible?

Catherine: And you always need to be dreaming bigger, right? Always be looking for the next step.

Lacey: Yeah. I read something or heard something recently, if your goal for your life isn't intimidating, if it doesn't scare you, then it's not big enough. If you feel comfortable with what you're dreaming about, then it's insulting to the universe, so to speak. It's always important to dream really big and have a stretch goal and be a little afraid and feel like you're taking a risk. That's really where you get your greatest reward.

Catherine: Love it. Very, very awesome tips that you've shared with us. There is one more thing that I would like to hear about because family is important to me. My family is my passion, and they are what drives me, and I love that you and your husband have made this, as you stated, a true family affair and you've incorporated your boys in building this dream of yours. You found ways that you can include them, and for them, it has to do with artwork. I would like to hear a little bit more about what that is.

Lacey: Sure. So we had, let's see…we started the winery…some people ask, "What were you thinking, having babies and starting a business at the same time?" I don't if we were thinking, but we decided just to do what we need to do and get started now. We have Francis who's going to be three and Eugene who's going to be five, both in December. I hope they don't take their childhood for granted growing up at a winery, but they love it. They know exactly what mommy and daddy do, that they make wine and work in a tasting room, out in the vineyard or the barrel house. Last year, we decided to involve our boys a bit more we started what we're calling an Artist Series. For all of our limited release or special release wines, we turn our boys' artwork into the labels.

It's so funny. The first label that we put on was from our older son, Eugene. He was like, "Why is my drawing on a wine bottle?" We said, "Because we think it's cool and we wanted to show everybody." Now he'll draw something, and he'll show it to me and say, "Mom, don't you think this will look great on a wine bottle?" Now they're trying to get their artwork on a label.

If you come into our tasting room, you will know that it's all about family. All of the pictures on the wall are pictures of our boys sitting on wine barrels; a picture of Francis and I planting one of the first rows of vines in our vineyard; a picture of my husband's great grandma who we named one of our wines after, who's turning 90 this year – super cute picture of her and our youngest son, Francis. You know it's all about family.

We teach our boys about the process as well, and it's so cute. When Eugene's out in the tasting room, he gets to be the businessman. He hands out business cards to everyone and makes sure everyone has a glass of water. He loves organizing the "selling table." We have a little bit of merchandise in a certain corner. He likes to organize that. I have to re-organize it, but I don't let him know that.

Francis, our youngest son, is on dad's heels out in the barrel house. He likes to ask, "Dad, what's this for? What do you do with this? What's in this barrel? What's in that barrel?" He is curious about the winemaking side. I know they're super young, and they'll probably change through the years, and of course the boys, can do whatever they want to do when they get older, but it would be the ultimate treasure to be able to pass this along to them; that would be amazing.

Catherine: Regardless of what they will do in the future when they grow up, the skills that you are teaching them are incredible. The confidence that you are giving them through incorporating them into this business and marketing and showing their artwork…what an incredible opportunity to build their confidence and to prepare them for the future for whatever they end up doing.

Lacey: Absolutely, yes. I hope that they know, "Mom and dad started this from scratch so that means I can go out and do anything."

Catherine: Definitely. Wonderful. It has been such a pleasure to speak with you and get to know you and the process that you've been through and the success that you've created. I love the many tips that you have shared; very great tips that many people will be able to glean from and be inspired by.

You said that you like to inspire people. Well, you have shared a lot of information, a lot of inspiring information.

Lacey: Thank you. I'm happy to be a part of it.

Catherine: You're welcome.

CHAPTER 12

Lindsay Andreotti

CEO- Brilliance Enterprises

You were born to win, but to be a winner you must plan to win, prepare to win and expect to win. ~ Zig Ziglar

Catherine: We are honored to have Lindsay Andreotti as our guest on the show today. Lindsay is the founder and CEO of Brilliance Enterprises, working with high school kids for their success through coaching and leadership. Lindsay has served as the Executive Director for Washington Future Business Leaders of America bringing with her many years of experience working with businesses around the world. Lindsay has assisted in the start, growth and development of over 200 companies, small and large, in both public and private sectors as well as for non-profit arenas. With a passion for coaching conscious leaders who want to "play to win" rather than "playing not to lose," Lindsay has focused her attention and the systems and psyche of the human side of the business to create significant results. Some of the companies she has mentored include Tommy Bahama, Coinstar, Microsoft, and hundreds of small to midsized businesses, earning from 50 thousand dollars up to 5 million dollars per year. She taught entrepreneurs at the University of Washington, Foster School of Business and Albers School of Business at Seattle University. She was co-director for Startup Washington from 2011 to 2013 and gave multiple speeches around Washington State on the subject of leadership and entrepreneurship to make

Washington great. As a serial entrepreneur, skilled coach, business advisor, strategist, and connector, she now focuses her passion on educating and mentoring next generation entrepreneurs for a better world. Welcome Lindsay, we're very excited to have you here!

Lindsay: Thank you, Catherine, I'm very excited to be here!

Catherine: I would like to hear a little bit about your teaching leaders how to "play to win" rather than "playing not to lose." What is the differentiation between that thought process?

Lindsay: That's a great question actually and thank you for noticing it; many people just gloss right over. The concept of playing to win is creating a life and being intentional about what you're doing so that you get more of what you love. A lot of people will focus on their life trying to hold onto what they have or trying to avoid losing something that maybe was important or perhaps that they felt like they should never deserve or shouldn't have received in the first place. So my work is around helping individuals get the mindset of how to win the game, define it and create a life that you love.

Catherine: I Love it! What a difference it can make when you change that mindset. When you look at that phrase "play to win" versus "play not to lose," to many people it would seem like the same thing, but in reality it isn't. It's all a matter of what you're focused on, right?

Lindsay: That's exactly right and it's fun because I don't usually use sports metaphors but I do have a son who plays lacrosse, and he is a defender, and we talk a lot about when you play life versus offense or defense, where's your focus? And it does make a huge difference. You still have a game to play on both sides of that, but if you're playing your game to win and to do the blocking and tackling that is required for the team to win, it's a very different mindset than playing to avoid losing.

Catherine: Absolutely. Lindsay, how did you get started in this industry?

Lindsay: Well, that's a great question. I spent a lot of years in my youth do-ing leadership roles and activities, so I probably got myself involved in far too many things way too many times.

Lindsay: In high school, myself, I was the person who couldn't stop doing pretty much everything. What I learned by that is that the field of overwhelm is quite large and for its use today it is even larger, because the opportunities are endless. What I noticed probably in the last ten years is that our next gen-eration of young people says from age 30 down to second grade right now, this generation is being called Generation Z. What's interesting about the 20-year-olds and down, which is true generation Z, they're a crossover be-tween Millennials and Generation Z; they are feeling like they are underuti-lized and becoming unmotivated and hopeless because of the current think-ing of the generations before them. I got a whiff of that when I was working at the University of Washington and Seattle U teaching entrepreneurship and noticing that our youth, our young people, were not willing to fail. They were playing life not to lose. And so I got motivated to do something about that and to listen to them. I spent the last decade truly using my time as much as I can to listen to entrepreneurs and leaders who are in this age group trying to make a difference in the world and figuring out where they get stuck and finding mentors and individuals to help them get unstuck. So that's how I got started, it's a long history of my life and the work that I've done over the last 30 years to get to this point, but that's really where I discovered in the last decade my true passion and where I want to focus my time.

Catherine: That's great! And you mentioned that long road that you've been down.

Catherine: Could you tell us a little bit about that and what kind of road-blocks you faced?

Lindsay: Absolutely! So I started my career really in about 1988 and got out of college and wasn't sure what I wanted to do specifically, but I knew I wanted to the work areas of either human resources or marketing. I knew that my passion was around people and I needed to figure out how people created profit in business. So I have an undergraduate business degree in international business and in about 1996, 94 to 96, I went back and got a master's degree in organization development, with the purpose of understanding whole systems thinking and how do you align people, profit, and process. That was my stick actually, I did that for years as a consultant, as an internal employee to other internal organizations. Some roadblocks that I met along the way we're, what's organization development? How do you know anything about technology and the business of technology if you worked in and name another kind of organization? That was probably one of my favorite stories, was when I went to go work for a wonderful start-up called Equator Technologies in about 1997. The CEO, bless his heart, John O'Donnell, loved the guy, he said to me "I don't know how in the world you can help us as a tech start up when you've worked most recently, you know, helping start-up cities." And I looked right at him, and I said, "John, I cannot program a multimedia processor, nor will I ever be able to, but I will be able to help you, A) find the people who can, B) motivate them to want to do it for you and C) keep them here so that they don't work for your competitor. That's what I do best."

Lindsay Andreotti: And he said, "You're hired." But it was a conversation of, you know, how does one person translate from one industry to another, to another when they don't have necessarily the technical background of whatever industry that is? What I've shown repeatedly is that it's not really about understanding the industry, it's about understanding people. Human beings are the common thread amongst all organizations, some of them more complicated than others. A few other stumbling blocks are things like cultural issues, not necessarily global cultural issues, but more, how do people work together in a tribe called an organization? I've met with some pretty ugly and toxic cultures that I was asked to help change or turn around, and that can be very challenging. You know, those are not easy tasks to do to get people to think differently than they currently think, especially when they've been operating in that environment for a long time. So, pretty difficult.

Catherine: So would you say that one of the biggest struggles that your clients face is their thinking process and getting beyond their beliefs that they already currently have?

Lindsay: Absolutely, that's one of them. It's able to stay open to the possibility that there is another way to work together or to do something differently and to achieve results. That is without a doubt a mindset issue. One of the challenges in that is that I think in our world today, we have a ton of books and research and information about how to change our minds and how our brains are starting to work.

Lindsay: The challenge is that many people are so afraid to change. They're not sure about what the brave new world looks like or how it might be better if they change their mind. So they play not to lose and that's a hard concept for many people to get over in today's environment, including our youth, it scares them.

Catherine: Oh! Change is a scary thing for many!

Lindsay: Indeed.

Catherine: So how do you help your clients get beyond that fear of change?

Lindsay: Awesome, that's one of my favorite questions. One of the things that I noticed about change is there was a company that I started back in the year 2000 with some colleagues of mine, and it was called Raven Fire, and our tagline was "if you can see it, you can do it." Well, what I've noticed is that that has been a true tagline for my entire life. One of the things that I believe helps someone change their mindset is when they can get heart connected to a vision that they actually can see. It's not just a pipe dream like, oh yeah, I'd like to be a world class surfer, you know, whatever. Yay! But they honestly can feel it in their body, in their bones, that one of the pieces of their life that they're attempting to create is something they can visualize. It's when a person can see what is possible, the experience of going to that place and what their life would be like when they can change to that. Suddenly all of the roadblocks start to move, and the brain begins to rewire towards that new reality, and it's a matter of taking them to a place of clarity of their vision. For some people and I'm not, you know, Pollyanna to the max here.

Lindsay: For some people, it's very difficult to envision anything differently than what is. For those individuals, I work on things like take them back to the past. Well, what did you dream about when you were a kid? Or I can take them forward, imagine the world for your grandchildren. When they can get out of their current situation enough and spend a little time digging deeper, many people can find a future that will work. One of my favorite examples of this, in reality, is a student of mine that I worked with last year who was a high school senior, was applying to college and had a litany of colleges he wanted to go to. He's an intelligent young man wanting to study computer science and engineering and his dream was to go to Stanford, but he didn't believe he could go. He applied to many other schools; he did apply to Stanford. I wrote him a letter of recommendation for Stanford, and I sat down with him one day, and I say, Dylan, here's the thing, I want you to visualize yourself on the Stanford campus. I want you to visualize what it is you'd be working on and how that might be life changing for you if you got to be there. About two months ago, he got a letter from Stanford that said he was wait listed as a candidate for the fall and one month ago he sent me a video of him receiving the letter that said: "you have been officially accepted to the Stanford Cardinal."

Catherine: Wow! That's incredible!

Lindsay: Incredible! He honestly did not believe. He's a little kid, not little, he's 6 foot 6, he's a kid from a very small town actually in Washington that is going to Stanford because he could visualize something that he didn't see possible before.

Catherine: Wow, how amazing. Lindsay, you obviously can make a great impact on many people, and I'm very impressed by what you do, and I love how you have taken your roadblocks and you've just crushed them to get to where you're at, and you are now implementing those skills to teach others how to do the same thing. I just want to ask you one more question. You've talked about your journey a little bit - what would you say was the biggest factor that contributed to your current success?

Lindsay: I'll give you the short answer first and then I'll expand. The short answer is I had a wonderful support network, friends, family, partners, who believed in me and what I was doing. And number two is every time I would get stuck, I would reach out to my mentor, coach, guide, friend, colleague, whoever, to remind me of what it was that I said I was doing and what I was up to, to stay on the path. So I think the key to my success has been surrounding myself with amazing people and never being afraid to ask for what I needed when I got totally jammed up. And I think that as human beings that's a really good lesson for all of us. It's difficult to ask for support or to ask for what we want because we feel like we're needy or we're not strong enough, or we didn't do right or whatever. The reality is, no, none of that's true. People want to help you more than you know and when we ask, it gives them an opportunity to share their love, kindness, wisdom, whatever we need at that moment. So I will 100% attribute my success to that.

Catherine: That is a beautiful message for our listeners, and it really goes to show it doesn't matter where you are at in your life or your career, whether you're beginning or whether you've built up a great successful business, there is always something more to learn, there is always more mentoring and more coaching that we can seek for, always. Always! Wonderful! Thank you, Lindsay. Are there any last comments that you would like to share before we finish the show?

Lindsay: You know, my only comment is this - do what you love and be who you are. That is the recipe for success for anyone, and it sounds to me, Catherine like you're doing that as well in your life and I'm certain that all of the other people that you will talk to will say some version of that. That is the key to being the very big success that you belong on this planet. So, thanks for making the time today.

Catherine: You're welcome! Thank you so much for being on the show.

Lindsay: You're very welcome!

CHAPTER 13

Marla Williams

CEO- Practical Solutions Zone

Get out of your head and get into your greatness. ~ Les Brown

Catherine: We're very privileged to have Marla Williams on the show today! Marla is the CEO of Practical Solutions Zone. She a is life, career, and business coach; however, Marla is not just your average life career and business coach, she is a pioneering visionary who has experienced tremendous success as a key leader in helping create a culture that grew a $12 million company into a $2.3 billion global corporation. She intuitively knew that she was meant to do more in this world and went on to create her legacy by building her own successful coaching business. Marla's gifts are her innovative spirit and her innate ability to know exactly what to focus on to be able to guide her clients through a personal transformation where they are creating their legacy or if leaders in the work world, creating game-changing cultures that exist long after they are gone. Whether you are an individual thinking there must be more to life or a business leader, or company owner knows you want to make a bigger difference in the world... listen in. Marla has a lot to share with us today, and we're very excited to hear what she has to share. Marla, thank you for being on the show. Please tell us a little bit about your company.

Marla: I founded Practical Solutions in 2012, and as you mentioned in the introduction, I provide life, career, and business coaching. When I first ventured into coaching, I found that I would start to work with someone on their career and a lot of life issues would come up, or if I were coaching an individual in business, life issues would surface or they might decide they wanted to change careers because they've finally found themselves or really discovered what it is that they're passionate about. As a result, I provide all three disciplines intermixed together. I am fortunate enough that my life experiences provided me with the skills and knowledge to be able to do that. My focus is to help people find peace, purpose, and prosperity in their lives whether it be in life, career or business.

Catherine: Beautiful. Those tie in together and I have found too that when someone is having a struggle in their business, it's usually because of something that came up in their life, something that they are struggling with personally, so I love how you tied those three things together.

Marla: You are so right! I have also come to realize that a big piece of the equation is the mindset. How you operate in the world is based on how you're thinking. It affects how you're reacting to life, and it's, often a result of things that you have faced in your life and your internal belief system.

Catherine: So what are you most passionate about in your role?

Marla: Teaching people how to get out of their heads, or out of their hole, or out of their stuckness and into their hearts. It is based on a basic philosophy I have. I believe that people are born with natural intuition. Watch a one or two years old follow their heart; they do what they love. If a child is more interested or naturally inclined to be athletic, they're going to be drawn to the balls and playing outside a lot when they're very young. If a child's heart sings when they build little blocks and that type of thing, they may end up being an engineer or in a career where they get to solve problems. When you watch a one or two-year-old, they tend just to gravitate to what they like, and if it's taken away from them, they get upset. As they grow up and start to go to school, all of a sudden, instead of just doing what they love and following their heart, they have to start following the rules, making their teacher happy while keeping their parents happy by getting good grades and that's when they go in their heads and listen more to that little voice in their head than their heart. That's our culture. The majority of the people I coach are what I call stuck in their heads because we've been brought up that way, with a belief system that encourages actions that support pleasing others or achieving success more than creating happiness by listening to your own heart. I have seen so many cases of young people who moved from listening to their hearts to trying please everybody else. As kids get older, about ten or twelve, they start paying attention to what everybody else is wearing and thinking. They are trying to fit in, and they're trying to be liked, and so they go more and more away from what naturally makes them happy and try to be popular or be liked. That's when people begin to go through a lot of struggle and lack confidence because they are paying more attention to that voice in their head that is causing doubt or self-confidence issues. This happens a lot between age ten and age fifteen. When they finally reach high school, some people are fortunate enough to follow still what they love, but there are many kids that struggle at this point because they've gotten so good at just trying to fit in and be liked that they're no longer listening to their intuition. So what I'm most passionate about, as you can see, is teaching people how to get out of their head, out of their stuckness and out of trying to fit in. Instead, I teach them to listen to their heart, their inner wisdom or their intuition. I have some great tools to help them practice so they become very good at listening to their inner wisdom, and listening to their feelings so that they can pull out of unhappiness or stuckness and begin to move into a life they love or start transforming their lives into one that they want.

Catherine: Do you have an example of how you go about getting somebody out of their head so that they can begin to listen to their heart again?

Marla: Yes. One example is... let me just walk you through an experience so you, get a feel for what I'm talking about. Is that okay with you?

Catherine: Sure, go ahead.

Marla: Okay. So basically it's your body, your biology, your system knows what is best for you. If you cut your finger, your body naturally begins to heal that wound. This is no different. Our body, our heart knows what is best for us. It is our intuition. We're born with that ability. That is what you see in very young children who are happily doing what speaks to their heart. What we do is we start living in our heads or listening to that little voice in our heads, which I call ego. What I do brilliantly is taught people how to start listening to their heart (or inner wisdom) again. Do you have pets by chance? A dog or cat?

Catherine: I have a cat.

Marla: Is it a cat that you love or is it persnickety?

Catherine: Yes, yes, he is a big part of the family.

Marla: So your cat is your focus as we go through this exercise. The reason I bring up cat or dog is that pets love you unconditionally no matter what. When you think about them, your heart usually will warm because no matter what you do or say, if you're having a tough day, your cat will be there at your side purring. Your dog will be greeting you with excitement, and you do no wrong. A baby is the same way. If you have a young child or a baby and when they're just so happy and looking at you with unconditional love; it's that warm feeling. Can you feel the warmth in your heart when I'm talking about this?

Catherine: Absolutely.

Marla: So that's what I do is I teach people how to warm up their heart and then, I have them ask yes/no questions. In your case warm up your heart thinking of a pet, child, whatever it is that makes your heart really warm - things you love to do, and when it's nice and warm I want you to say, "My name is Catherine."

Catherine: My name is Catherine.

Marla: And your heart's going to stay warm. Now say, "My name is Susie."

Catherine: My name is Susie.

Marla: And your heart's going to cool. When you say truth statements, your heart will warm or stay warm. When you say false statements, your heart will always cool. What people quit doing is listening to their heart, listening to that warmth. When you get good at getting your heart warm and then asking yes/no questions and following the feeling, following the warmth, warmth is always truth or yes; when it cools off, it's a no or an untruth. I have a lot of different tools that I use to help people with this, and there are different tests (biology - your body knows what's right) that you can do - sway tests, muscle testing, etc., but there's a lot of different backup tests that are very, very accurate. When you learn to listen to that warmth to your body, to your feelings, to your intuition your life will change, absolutely in front of you. There is more to this, people live in what I call their ego head, and it's based on a lifetime of things they've heard and experienced within their culture, or based on family beliefs, what parents have said, what your teachers have said or what your coaches or other key influencers have said. We were brought up being conditioned by the people and events in our lives, and we believe that is our truth. Often, our head is an incessant stream of compulsive thoughts that doesn't turn off. We may think and say, "Oh I should do this," or "I won't do this," or... I can't do this. You begin to identify with your story that you created from your life experiences. It becomes your habits, and it becomes your way of being. What I do is I help people get in touch with that part of them, I help them understand what is their ego, or their subconscious or unconscious because that part of them is controlling their life. We have, in my, in my opinion, three brains. We have a brain, a heart brain, and a gut brain. The head brain is your conscious brain which we're only using like five or ten percent of its potential. It is where your logic, your problem solving, your ability to understand science and your math capabilities reside. The 2nd brain is your heart brain. Your heart brain sends more messages to your head brain than your brain sends to your heart and they've proven this scientifically. The heart brain, in my opinion, is your intuition - it's able to listen to and follow your heart, your ability to follow your feelings. The brains you want to listen to when making any decisions is your heart brain along with your conscious brain. Your gut brain is your warning system, kind of that fight or flight feeling. If you're in a dangerous situation, you start clenching in your gut and you know something's off. That's used more rarely and in more of a life-saving type of situation. Going back to the heart - what I do is teach people to live there and how to turn off the ego or little voice in your head. The other 90% to 95% of your head brain is stuck in this subconscious-unconscious ego, and it's that piece of you that doesn't benefit you. It might be emotions, patterns and belief systems based on your upbringing. Things that are ego include Worry, anxiety, stress, boredom, despair, satisfaction. All those things are ego; fear is ego, and a TON of people have it. There are patterns that show up in people's lives whether it's a shame, or complaining, or blaming, or needing to be a liked or, judgment. It's those type of things that show up, and they are patterns originating from your ego. There are belief systems, "should've, would've, could've," powerless, feeling unworthy, not enough, not good enough...all of those things are part of this ego. That's the tougher part - helping people learn to let go of those beliefs, shut down that voice in their head and learn to follow and listen to their heart instead.

I can do this effectively because I learned this first hand. I was stuck in my head even though I always had a natural intuition. I got stuck in my head when after a very successful corporate career we sold out to a Fortune 500 which cleared out all the long term employees so all of a sudden I'm out on the street going, "What am I going to do next? This has been my life, and it was such a wonderful company." What am I qualified to do? Who will want to hire me? I started going into my head; I got stuck in a poor me mentality while trying to figure it out. I applied to other companies and started to interview, but nothing felt right. I got offers. I got opportunities but nothing that got me excited. I knew that there might not be a lot of companies out there that were as awesome as the company that I worked for and helped grow. As a result of nothing feeling right...I started questioning whether I could find a company and job that I would love. Your thoughts become your reality. I was focused on thinking I wouldn't find it and I didn't. The good news, I made a decision at that point to move into a coaching career, so it all worked out better than ever. The point I want to make here. is what you focus on becomes your reality. If you are having good things happen to you, you think positive thoughts, and you get caught up in a positive spiral, and everything's good, and you feel wonderful. When things don't feel right or good, you begin to feel more stuck in your life, and you start going into the negative spiral.

So beyond teaching people to listen to their heart and get out of their head, I help them begin to focus on what they do want and not what they don't want because that helps move them forward. That was MY biggest roadblock, and that's usually one of the biggest roadblocks for my clients. It's this three part series of getting out of your head, into your heart, and focusing on what you do want.

147

Catherine: So you talked about when you made that transition from your job, having lost that job, and you got stuck in YOUR head, and there was a process that you went through to come about doing what you do. At what point did you realize that coaching was in your heart and how did you how did you get started on that?

Marla: So when I was first put out to pasture, at first it was the "oh my gosh" and then the painful process of creating a resume and applying, and on top of the feeling that nothing felt right. I kept saying to myself... "What do I want to do?" and the answer came to me in an unexpected way. I was listening to a webinar at that time with a lot of inspirational speakers. The company putting this webinar on offered a free weekend workshop for anyone that wanted to come. Everything in this inspirational radio show was speaking to me. For the first time since the layoff, my heart was singing. I was listening to this, and I went to my husband and said, "I have to go to this weekend event. I have to see what it's about." He wanted me to be happy so agreed. I flew out to Colorado and went to this live event. It was a group of people that train people how to be energy coaches. They teach them how to listen to their energy, how to listen to their intuition and I was so drawn to it all. It just spoke to my heart, so I ended up signing up for one of their courses. The reason they bring you down is to get you to sign up of course...and so I did, but everything from my very first day in the training felt right. Everything about it spoke to me, and I was like a duck to water. It felt like I had come home and I just knew it, I intuitively knew it was what I was meant to be doing and learning. They had a two-year certification program and because of my strong background in business and Human Resources where I had been coaching and counseling and training people for years and I had already had a lot of natural ability. Their coaching training was a two-year program yet because everything just made sense and it clicked, I got through the program in six months, and I started coaching people that had been in the program longer than me, and they were blown away. They asked me questions like "Are you a psychic, are you have a hypnotist?" And I wasn't, it was just everything about the program and training spoke to me at a deep level. I learned to reconnect with my intuition, follow what I was feeling and my life just has turned around as a result. Now I teach my clients how to do just that.

Catherine: Wow, that's very incredible! Beautiful story, and just beautiful how you came about this, how you went through that process. Clearly, you are in the right place.

Marla: I'm doing exactly what I'm meant to be doing, and that's so key for people. When you find that one thing that just opens up your heart and makes you feel good and makes your heart sing, you know...you just keep following that.

Catherine: We can hear, Marla, that your heart is singing.

Marla: It is.

Catherine: Thank you, is there anything else that you would like to share with us as far as what you do and how you can help assist people with getting through their roadblocks. I know you've covered quite a bit, is there anything that you may have missed.

Marla: Yeah, there's one other thing that I do that is unique, and I think it's important to share this. I do offer my coaching one-on-one, but what I have found in all the years that I've done the coaching are there are many people in circumstances and situations where they've gone into that negative spiral, they're stuck in their heads, and they don't have the money to coach one-on-one. I believe that everybody should have the opportunity to be able to get coaching and to be able to move forward in their lives. I spent a lot of time thinking about this, and I created a program called "Loving Life" and that program is a group coaching that I offer for very, very low rate to help those people who might be stuck or struggling and give them the opportunity to get coaching. It's a group coaching but they can submit questions, specific issues, and I'll discuss it. I do a call every week and I record that call.

Catherine: Excellent, thank you very much, Marla, for sharing this with us today.

Marla: You're welcome, thank you for having me, Catherine.

CHAPTER 14

Ruth Nicholson

Manager- Nicholson facilitation and Associates LLC

The quality of our lives depends not on whether or not we have conflicts,
but on how we respond to them. ~ Tom Crum

Catherine: We are very fortunate to have Ruth Nicholson with us today who is the manager of Nicholson facilitation and Associates LLC. She is also an internationally certified professional facilitator, visual and graphics facilitator, certified assessor and trained mediator in private practice in the Snohomish County, Washington area. She is also a member of the U.S. Institute for Environmental Conflict Resolution which is a federal roster of mediators. She holds a master's degree in public administration and offers over 25 years of experience in organizational development, facilitation, conflict resolution, public policy, and nonprofit organization management. Ruth has regularly served as both a lead facilitation and project manager responsible for project team management and staff supervision, meeting design and collaborative agenda development, document and meeting notes production, and project contracting timeline and budget. In addition to offering facilitation services, Ruth has provided facilitation training in North America as a one-on-one facilitation coach trainer and at international conferences in Africa, Asia, the Caribbean, Europe, and North America. She has also served as an international assessor evaluating candidates for professional facilitator certification in Africa, North

America, and Asia. Ruth Nicholson is the co-author of "When There are no Easy Answers... A Facilitator's Guide to Designing Complex Events" which is based on input from over 100 facilitators around the world and the article "Post Agreement Conflict: A Reflection of the Causes and the Development of Skills to Address It."

Welcome Ruth, we are very excited to have you with us today, and we would like to hear more about what it is that you do. It sounds like you do so much; it sounds pretty complex.

Ruth: Well thank you, Catherine. I'm glad to be here with you. Really, at its simplest, it's about people, organizations and getting results. When you boil all of it down, I sort of have three areas of practice. I have my teaching and training; in that component, I really enjoy giving people practical skills, simple things they can do that make it easier to work with the people in the organization so that they actually can deliver on the kinds of programs that are near and dear to their hearts. I like practical training. My mother used to call every time I had a new client and say, "Well are they going to be better off next week than they were last week?" That was the bar.

The second part of my practice has traditionally been in the area of environmental issues and natural resource issues where there's often a fair amount of conflict. You have multiple organizations, multiple agendas and a unique mix of technical and scientific along with the values that people bring to natural resources and environmental issues; and again it's about helping bring people work either within their organization or across organizations to do things with the environment that are good for community and good for the environment.

The third piece of my practice is actually all of that - what I call in a different color jersey because it has a lot to do with children and youth sports and again working with organizations, many of whom have lots of volunteers, a lot of parent volunteers, and they're trying to get their organization to work well to deliver on good experiences for their kids. Again it's about people learning how to work together so that they can get stuff done, so your meetings are more productive, your programs are targeted, and when you have to have those difficult conversations you can actually have them and still have a good working relationship, and still produce the kind of programs that are important to you.

Catherine: Wow, thank you for summarizing that in a more simplistic fashion. That sounds fabulous. Ruth, how did you come about getting into this field of work?

Ruth: I like to call myself the accidental facilitator because if you had told me when I was in junior high or high school or even college, "When you grow up you're going to be a facilitator," I would have said well what the heck is a that. It's in my DNA I think because I grew up in a family where most of the men in the family were clergy or Scottish Presbyterian which meant that everybody's house had a committee in the living room; my grandfather and my father and my uncles...I mean everybody. So a survival skill in my family was working with people and groups. I didn't realize until I was well into my 30s that that skill of working with people in groups is not something that most people grow up with, but in my household, that's what my mom did, and my dad did, and my grandma did. I was working as a forester. My first university degree is in forest science, and most foresters don't go into forestry to talk to people. We had a huge controversy here in the Northwest around the spotted owl, and the issue was how do you manage the woods with the spotted owl in it? Whether you were a timber company or the federal government or state government or tribe, it generated a whole lot of conflict, and I was laid off not once but twice because Foresters were losing their jobs by the drove. I ended up at the Federal Environmental Protection Agency, and they sent me back to facilitate a group at the Forest Service which was all about how do we manage the woods with the spotted owl in it? All of a sudden the things that my mother had taught me unconsciously as a little kid were what was making a difference for those people in that room and trying to resolve the issues, both technical and value based, around the issue of how do you manage woods in the Pacific Northwest? That then became a career in facilitation and mediation. Over time I was with the federal government and some private consulting firms, and I ended up out on my own. Sort of the last piece of the story, well up to date, is when I had kids, I have two sons, and they played sports they were soccer nuts and all of a sudden as a volunteer soccer clubs will come me and say, "You know, we're having trouble with our board of directors or we're having trouble with this contract, could you help us? You do it over there, could you do it over here?" All of a sudden that blossomed into not quite a second career, maybe it's my third career, in helping youth sports organizations avoid some of the heartaches from the pitfalls of parent conflicts and pushing kids to excel too soon. It's really at the younger ages where learning the skill and learning to love the sport take place. I think it's just the family DNA and a different color jersey.

Catherine: I can see that. You honed in on using your experience, the things that you learned and recognizing your talents and it sounds like you take that into what you do. You're talking about the youth in sports and not pushing them but rather helping them to realize where their skills are and helping them to expand on those skills. Would you say that's correct?

Ruth: Yeah, and it's the same theme whether you're talking about scientists and nuclear waste at the Hanford Nuclear Reservation or whether you're talking about the Little League and how do we help kids who are who are going through puberty and going through that clumsy stage that we all have gone through and still retain a love of the sport and a love of athletics and being physically active? It's helping people play to their strength and be successful doing that.

Catherine: Yeah, absolutely and I can see where that playing to your strengths it can be anywhere; in sports, in your organization, your communities. Beautiful, so as you went through this journey to get to where you're at what are some of the roadblocks that you faced?

Ruth: One of the roadblocks I've always faced is being female. I come from a family of mostly males. I don't have sisters. I have one female cousin out of a dozen cousins I have. I'm a title nine kid and we were not allowed to play sports when I was a kid in North Texas and we had we had a small little fight about how, yes, girls can play soccer, and I was one of the first soccer referees and assignors. I guess it was groundbreaking. I went to forestry school. Forestry school was not full of women even now although when I went in the late 70s early 80s, there were even fewer of us and even now I work with scientists and engineers and a lot of coaches, a lot of athletic coaches, all of those are fields that are traditionally more male than female.

I think the another challenge has been that what I do isn't flashy; it isn't a magnet for attention. Heck, it's not even sexy. It's useful, and it's valuable but helping people see that is also a challenge that it doesn't have to be that hard. What I do is a lot like being a referee in a sporting match, right? If the referee does a good job, you don't notice the referee is there. You know, you're watching the game you're cheering for your team, nobody gets hurt, hey this is great. If the ref screws up then, everybody notices the ref and has an opinion about it. I think as a facilitator it's very much like that because if you ace that piece of work, if people come together and they come to an agreement, they design a great program, you can tell as they leave the room. The energy level will be high; it won't be that dragging, "Oh gosh I've been in this meeting all day and all we can do is to get out of here," but they'll leave the room, and there will be a buzz. I mean, literally, the energy will be high, and you'll hear people say "Did you see what we did, we're really looking forward to following up next week or doing this thing," and your name won't be in the sentence as the person who designed that process or facilitated that meeting or helped them reach that play. They own it, and it's theirs, and they're excited, and they're proud of it. You know you've done a really good job, but the challenges are since your name is not in that sentence from a marketing standpoint or a "Do you remember that you had some help getting there?" That's always a little bit of a challenge because you're often the afterthought. Even though what you've done is make it possible for them to come together and be successful. That's a perennial. It's sort of like inviting people over to supper and you cook a great meal and set the table and it's really pretty and the atmosphere is great and you can't make them eat but if they do eat, and they, do have fun they'll remember the people in the party; they might not remember some the foundational stuff that made that happen but it's still a great meal.

Catherine: Absolutely. How do you overcome that sense of not getting the recognition that you deserve? How do you work with that and find the strength to keep going and to recognize the value that you're offering for these people?

Ruth: Some days are easier than others. I think you have to have confidence in yourself. There's a genuine caring that lives within the people that do this sort of work and so there's celebration in other people's success. For example, with my sports stuff I have different coaches and different directors of coaching that I work with and I will make the time to see them and their teams when they play. It surprises people, but it makes an impression that helps them remember you when they need you. Two examples: one, a little more than a year ago, a year and a half maybe, I was going to visit my son who now lives in Arizona, and I had a coach that I had worked with online for a while and he had a little girl's team who was playing their last game of soccer for the season, and I said, "Hey, I'm going to be in Arizona are your girls playing?" He said, "Yes, they're playing on Friday night," and I said, "Well, I'm flying in on Friday can my son and I come watch your girls?" He said, "You don't know them." I said, "Well, I know you, and it's about supporting the children, right?" I never met him in person and my son, and I caught an Uber and went out to the soccer field and cheered for his girls. He was like, "You flew in from Washington State and the first thing you did after you had left the plane was come to watch my girls?" I said, "Well the point is supporting our kids."

In a couple of weeks I have a community college coach that I befriended at a coaching course and he's having some challenges with coaching young women who are just out of high school, just entering college and making that whole life's transition from "I live at home to now I'm in charge of like my whole schedule". He said, "Would you come out," and I'm like, "Yeah." I'm going to spend a whole day with him. In September they have a jamboree and it's, about a four-hour drive from where I am, and I'm like, "Yeah, I'll come out. You want me to cheer for your girls? We'll be there." Turns out one of the other coaches I'm working with is the opposing team coach. I had a lot of young women to cheer on that day; I can't lose that game.

It's about being present and caring and finding ways to show that, so when those folks say, "You know what? I have an organizational challenge," they know who to call, and they know who to trust, and I get a kick out of seeing them successful.

Catherine: So the big key for you is building connections. Wonderful! As you are building connections and you're working with these people what kind of roadblocks do you see them facing as your clients?

Ruth: I think one of the biggest roadblocks people have regardless of what field they're in is they will stay in uncomfortable, painful situations for incredibly long periods of time because they're more afraid of change than they are of the pain that they're currently living in. What are some of the challenges that my clients face? I think one of the biggest challenges they face, regardless of what field they're in, no matter what program or organization they work with, is finding themselves in a place where it's uncomfortable and painful and yet being more afraid of change and what that could look like as compared to just staying in the current pain. They'll choose current pain over the risk or the uncertainty of making a change to something they can't quite imagine. Helping people see, yes I'm acknowledging your pain, I understand that it's uncomfortable and it doesn't have to be that way. That with small steps, simple tools, practical techniques, you can make the situation better for yourself, for your organization, for the people who you're serving. Sometimes they have to go very small and very slow, and I get privately kind of impatient with that. But it has to work for them. People are going to do things for their reasons not for your reasons even if you think it's the greatest thing since sliced bread. They've got to do it for their reasons and so helping find their interests and how to satisfy those which is not only the secret to building good programs, it's the secret to mediation. You find people's interest, and you find different ways to satisfy those interests, and it can work like magic.

Catherine: Absolutely. Great point that you've made there. The important thing that I heard is that people will do things for their reasons and being able to come in and listen and find out what it is that their needs are, what it is that their wants are, and being able to work with them. I also really appreciate that you were very open and authentic in saying that sometimes it can be a small and slow process and you can get a little frustrated with that, yet you also recognize the importance of that and that you can set yourself aside and set aside what it is that you want; set aside the excitement that you have and perhaps a great idea that you have, and that's not always easy. That is a great skill to have.

Ruth: Ultimately if a solution is going to stick whether it's in your program or a mediation you have to own it because you're the one that has to live with it. So ultimately it doesn't matter what I think because I'm not the one living with it. When I was working on the paper on post-agreement conflict, we looked at some the factors that lead to the conflicts reemerging and looking at relationships with people and are you doing it for your reasons or somebody else's reason? I used to teach conflict resolution to third graders because at the elementary school across the street from my house every classroom had a peace table in the corner, and that's where kids could go to resolve issues, and if two children were having difficulty they could ask a teacher to help them or them could ask a fifth grader, because the fifth graders had their little student mediation cadre. So we started teaching the kids in third grade how to solve conflicts so when they were fifth graders they were pretty hot stuff. The whole nugget revolves around the story around an orange. I would show up in class with one orange, and I would get two kids help me. I would say, "Hey I have an orange, does anybody want the orange?" These two students would be, "Oh, yes yes, we want the orange." They would come up, and I would say, "Uh oh I only brought one what should I do?" Then the class would tell me to cut it in half. On cue the two little kids who are in on it, both of them would be unhappy. Cutting it in half was not an acceptable solution. I would look back at the class and I say, "What am I going to do now, they don't like that idea." Then there would be quiet, and being quiet is always a little tough, right? I would be quiet, and they would squirm and squirm and squirm, and you could feel the discomfort, right? We now have conflict over the orange. Finally, somebody would say, "Why do they want the orange?" Well, we didn't ask that question, so I asked one of the kids, "Why do you want the orange?" He would say, "Oh I'm hungry and I want all the orange because I'm really hungry." I'd say, "Well that's a pretty good interest." Then I would look at the other little one and say, "Why do you want the orange?" He would say, "Well, it's my daddy's birthday and his favorite cake is orange, and I want to grate the orange peel to help make his birthday cake." The little ones would get it. If I ask, "Why is this important to you?" I start getting behind the position, so if your position is I want the orange, your interest is I'm hungry, your interest is I'm baking a cake, and the magic of working with people is to get beyond the position, "I want this," to "Why is that important to you?" Is it respect, is it profit for the company, is it service to young basketball players...why is that important to you? Once you start uncovering that there are a whole lot of different ways to share that orange and you can end up with people happier with the solution than if you did the obvious which is, "Oh, we're just going to cut it in half."

Catherine: Oh I love that! That is an incredible example. I love it! What an empowering message that you can give to these young children in conflict resolution, that is just incredible.

Ruth: It's all about asking, "Why?" It sounds simplistic, but even as an adult you know you find yourself in a conundrum with your spouse or your child or somebody you work with and stopping and saying, "Wait a minute, I need to understand something. Why is this important to you (not to me; I know why it's important to me)? Why is it important to you? What is it about this thing?" I know when I'm a conflict I tend to lead with my why and people don't always get it and I'll find myself saying, "It's important to me because...." The position isn't enough information, at least not for me. When I'm dealing with something, even if it's not conflict...say it's an organization and a committee, and they're designing a new program for what they do and getting underneath, "We want to build this program," well, what is it about that program that's really important? What's the result you want? Is it an experience? Is it an outcome? Why is that so near and dear to your heart? When you have an agreement around that, people will rally and make it happen. That's what I do for a living.

Catherine: That's wonderful. I love that, and I can see that you have a great skill in being able to work with people on this level, and what a difference that you're able to make in the world by bringing these tools into these groups; these youth sports and these various organizations that you work with.

Ruth: Thank you. It helps if you like what you do.

Catherine: You know, it certainly does. That is a big key - to be able to do what you like to do; to be able to follow your passion. I can see that you are passionate about that. I know you've shared a little bit about what you love and how you love to help other people, but really, if you were to choose the thing that you are most passionate about with what you do, how would you summarize that?

Ruth: I love to help people succeed. I remember when I realized I don't have a need to be the sage on the stage; I love being a guide on the side and it's okay if the spotlight is on other people because their success is a reflection of my success.

Catherine: Beautifully put, thank you. I love it! Ruth thank you so much for being on the show today and for sharing with us such wonderful tools that the listeners or readers can take from this and implement into their lives and in their businesses. I am excited for the difference that you being on this show can make in the lives of many others. Thank you so much.

Ruth: Thank you for having me.

Catherine: You are welcome.

CHAPTER 15

Sherry Zins Calvert

President- Keiretsu Forum Northwest

My best skill was that I was coachable.
I was a sponge and aggressive to learn. ~ Michael Jordan

Catherine: Welcome to the show. We are greatly honored to have with us today, Sherry Zins Calvert, a U.S. Army veteran. She is also a married mother of four and the co-founder and president of Keiretsu Forum Northwest.

Keiretsu is based in Seattle, Washington and is part of the largest global private equity investment network. Keiretsu Forum Northwest represents seven of the thirty-nine international chapters, with over three hundred fifty members out of fifteen hundred. In 2014, Keiretsu Forum Northwest facilitated over $32.2 million of early stage investment for thirty-seven companies. In 2015 Keiretsu Forum NW 43 million into 57 deals. Sherry is an active member of her community and remains an advocate for veterans. As an accomplished engineer and sales person, Sherry's professional experience began at the age of seventeen when she enlisted in the U.S. Army and served as a communications specialist in the Army where she held a top secret clearance position. She continued her career in engineering after her military service with positions at SpaceLabs Medical, Zetron, Honeywell, Boeing, Solectron, and Qualitel. Between 2003 and 2009, Sherry acted as the Washington

Counsel Director of membership development for the American Electronics Association (AeA) where she was consistently in the top three for national sales and retention. She went on to be Membership Development Manager for WTIA before joining Keiretsu Forum Northwest.

Sherry maintains her interest in engineering as a board member of Washington FIRST Robotics Board where she has been a regional judge for the FIRST Robotics Competition. She gives back through charitable organizations including the Yaletown House Foundation and the Alzheimer's Association. In 2015, she participated in Celebrity Waiters to raise money for the Millionair Club Charity, a Seattle-based non-profit organization aimed at helping those in need achieve permanent jobs, stable housing, and necessary support. She also is involved in many other charitable organizations where she serves in various committee membership positions.

We are very honored to have such a wonderful individual with us today. Thank you, Sherry, for taking the time to be with us. How did you come up with the name Keiretsu? That sounds like a Japanese name, is that correct?

Sherry: It is. Hello, Catherine. Thank you for having me on your show. Yes, Keiretsu came from our founder, Randy Williams, down in the Bay Area. His partners are Japanese. Keiretsu means a group or a gathering of like-minded individuals that help each other grow, so Keiretsu Forum is a group of angel investors that help each other succeed and grow. It's a network of people that band together for the common good; that's where the term came from.

Catherine: That's beautiful. I love that meaning, and it's very fitting for sure. How did you come about getting involved with Keiretsu?

Sherry: Well, as the number one salesperson for the American Electronics Association, my job was to speak with all the high tech C.E.O.'s in the region and find out about their issues, whether it be H1B visas or education, or whatever they were passionate about and wanted us to lobby for on their behalf. Because I had the ear of all the C.E.O.'s, when Keiretsu was forming here in the Northwest, they asked me to help them bring on members. I obviously took the job, and I loved working with them as a volunteer. I brought on over one-third of their membership in the first few months while I was volunteering for them.

Catherine: That's very impressive. What do you like most about what you're doing? What are you most passionate about?

Sherry: What I'm doing with Keiretsu that I like is helping entrepreneurs succeed and helping investors make good investment decisions. We have the whole range from entrepreneur startup. We help them; we point them in the right direction; we have committees that try to help these guys and girls get started. If we're not right for them, we will point them to the right people. We coach them for many years, sometimes until they're ready to make their pitch for the A round and once they make their pitch then we help them get funding, and we help our investors pick the best sound deals. Seventy-eight percent of the companies that come through our doors get funded; that's unheard of. Last year we funded globally seventy-nine million and Keiretsu Forum Northwest region did forty-nine million of that. Out of thirty chapters worldwide, we did more than half the revenue.

Catherine: Wow, that's incredible.

Sherry: We're pretty happy to get companies started. It's fascinating to learn about all these new startups and technologies, and just be there to help them and get them started. I was there for that. It's fun.

Catherine: What do you think creates such a great success so that you were able to help so many people? Like you said, that is unheard of.

Sherry: It is. I think it's our team. Being ex-military, being an engineer, I run on metrics. A lot of the other chapter presidents are successful business people themselves, but they're not soldiers. So, I think that being a soldier, just running lean and mean, and spending the resources where needed to provide the right amount of support for the company. So for example, we look at four new companies a month, and forty-eight new deals a year that we fund or try to fund. I have a staff member for each section of the process. I pay out quite a bit more than half of our income in salary just so that we have the best staff - the best team possible. I have an amazing team of young master degree students that have come out of the master's program and they volunteer for me for usually up to a year, and then they get hired. So it is just a stellar team and just a solid process.

Catherine: As you started with this company and had grown your success, would you say that you had run up against any roadblocks?

Sherry: Yes. The demographic for angel investors is fifty-five-year-old white males; it's very difficult to be diverse. It's hard to break into finance, especially with an engineering degree (my background), and for them to trust that I could do the finance and do the deals and bring them the best quality deal flow that I could bring. It took quite a bit of time to convince them. Year over year, since I took over the company, we have been the top performing chapters in the world. I'm pretty happy with that that we were number one every year that we've been in business since I took over in 2010 with my business partner.

Catherine: How would you say that you overcame those roadblocks and were able to create that trust and respect?

Sherry: Our performance. Again, metrics, just performing, being able to point the finger and say, "Here's how much we funded; here's how many companies we funded; here's the metric for what we do." Just being very public about what we're doing and earning their trust year over year. It wasn't just a flash in the pan. We stayed under the radar for the first couple of years, and we just built the company up, because it was kind of in a hole when I took it over. When I took it over, we had very few members left, and we had a bad reputation in town. My business partner and I decided that we could fix this because it was the right thing to do. When we took it over, we just sat down and said, "Look we're just going to perform. We're going to honor all contracts, and we're going to perform. Once we perform for at least three years in a row, to be stable, we're going to come out with guns." So we did. We've now come out, and we do press releases announcing our success and providing the numbers to anyone who's willing to look at them so that we can stand by what we do.

Catherine: A couple of things I heard in what you said is that there was openness and you had a plan.

Sherry: Yeah, that helps - having a mission.

Catherine: So they need to have a mission. As you work with people and you're helping businesses startup, and you're providing funding for these businesses, what do you see as the most common roadblock that your clients or members come up against?

Sherry: Well, usually they're just not prepared, they haven't researched the market, or they don't have the sales pipeline cued up so we look at companies that have been in business for at least a year that have a product or service complete and they're looking for money to grow their business to that next level. We're not looking at new startups. We do help them in the earlier phases through some committees I can talk about later, but at the stage when they come to the forum, they have to meet those criteria. That's why we have such a high success rate at 75% because one out of the four usually will fail. It's due to many things. It could be that the team is set up incorrectly, they don't have the right sales team, they don't have the right marketing plan, or they don't have the right vision. There are many reasons that they can fail.

I think seven out of ten startups fail and that's a huge statistic. Only seven percent of our investments account for 75% percent of our returns. There are other competitors that come out faster, stronger and better. There are many reasons for a startup to fail. We do 40 to 100 hours of due diligence on each of these companies that come through; we work with them; we coach them; we help them all along the way,so by the time they get to the forum they're ready and the only businesses that are not successful will be either they found money somewhere else, the company imploded, or they found out that what they're working on, just through the due diligence process, wasn't viable at this time and so they go back, reconfigure, and then come back a couple of years later.

We had a company, a very successful company, called Tilted Motor Works that we've been working with for five years. The first year they came through they weren't ready. We told them they weren't ready and we told them why. They went to fix it then came back a couple of years later, and they pitched. They were hugely successful, and they're doing great now.

Being able to tell them what's wrong and guide them, and for them to be coachable, as we all call it. Are they coachable? Will they listen and will they pivot? We know what will be successful, not necessarily what's going to make it, but we know the roadblocks that will stop them from making it.

Catherine: What I hear is that when somebody comes to you for assistance you do your due diligence to make sure that they're in the right place, that they have a proper plan, and then you spend a lot of time coaching them.

It sounds like you give them the tools or the guidance to let them go off on their own and take care of what they need to do and then they can later come back when they're better prepared and then you then can help them out. Is that correct?

Sherry: Yes, but we don't do a deep dive into the due diligence until they've made it into the forum. We will coach them on the side. We have what we call committees. I have ten committees - the space committee, life science committee, hardware Committee, and other different committees that will coach them as a committee as a sector group before they're ready for Keiretsu, but once they come to us, we then do the deep dive. That's when my investors know what they're investing in. We don't charge them a penny until they come to the actual forum, so all the coaching for years before doesn't cost them anything; that's us building the pipeline for the future. We provide a lot of help and guidance to help these companies, then they do pay to come to the forum and pitch, but again 75% of those get funded. That's the key - that we do what we say we're going to do.

Catherine: OK. Wow, that's pretty amazing that you do that and you provide such a great service.

Sherry: Thanks.

Catherine: You said that you work people that have been in business for at least a year and they have certain criteria that they meet. If you've got businesses that come to you that have been in business for less than a year, is that when you would put them in a committee and give them coaching?

Sherry: Exactly.

We will put them in a committee for coaching which doesn't cost them anything, or we will pass them onto another angel group that works with earlier stage companies. A lot of the angels like to work with the seed stages, any-thing under five hundred thousand. If they're just a start up, they go to their friends and family; they raise the money they can raise - that's a seed stage company. We're dealing with A round companies which are still startups, but they've got some traction. They have a product, like I said, that is already built; they have some customers that want what they have, it's not just "if we build it they will come," and they go on from there. It's a pretty good pro-cess. We have written books about our process. We share our due diligence process with all the other angel groups, and we have a very open policy, like I said, because we want everyone to be successful. The more companies that are funded, the better for the economy and everyone in general. I allow all the other angel group leaders to come to my forum and take deal flow and people are very surprised about that. They come, and they watch my pitches, and if they want to take them in their groups, I'm very happy for them; I al-low them to do that, which surprises a lot of different groups that are private.

Catherine: OK, I see. A lot of people who are reading this are individuals that are in the startup phase. Some of them are more established, but the goal in providing this book is to help them - to offer advice and encouragement not to give up. It's so easy, especially in the early stages of business, to give up when things don't go well; when things just don't go right or things don't go the way we think they should. There are all kinds of roadblocks that we all face in that phase. What kind of insight might you have for these people?

Sherry: Honestly, get in front of angel groups early. Get in front of us. You can come and pitch to my company or to any other angel group at what we call a deal screening. Now that is before we put you in front of the main group of investors, but go out there and get your deal screened. Don't be so paranoid about, "Oh my gosh, it's a top secret, super secret sauce and we're going to give it away." We don't ask that detail of questions. We are looking at do you have marketing? Do you have investors? Is it unique? Is it a cool idea? Do you have any IP or IP protection? You know, those things are what we're looking for, we are not looking for your deep secrets, we're looking for the overall do we believe it's viable? Do we believe in the team and do we think that you can get there? The quicker you get in front of groups, and they start screening you and giving you feedback, the quicker you're going to find out whether it's viable and a viable product and if people are going to invest in it. It's kind of like Shark Tank. I love that show because even though they're brutal on the show (you know, made for T.V.) they're like, "No one is going to buy this," and the entrepreneur might go away and think, "Wow, I've just been shot down." It's better to be shot down in the beginning when you're starting and work on something. Most groups don't do that by the way; we're very friendly, and we would never say that. We'd say. "Look, here's what we think you might change to make it more effective." So we call ourselves the dolphin tank.

You want to get that feedback so you can be prepared just to make that right decision and make those pivots before you come and ask for real money. People are shy and the biggest hurdles I think is thinking that their thing is this top secret that they can't let anyone know about and someone is going to steal it. Nobody is going to steal it in the angel group, they're just not, that's not who we are. Most angels are there to help the entrepreneur. Now they may tell you there are three other companies doing the same thing; it's probably a good idea to listen and research it and make sure that there are not three other companies doing the same thing that have more money than you to get it to market. No one wants to hear that. They all think it's all very special, and it is to them, but that's probably one of the worst parts of my job is that I don't like to break people's hearts or dash people's dreams, but I ask them the question in the end, would you rather I told you this now or two years down the road when your house is in debt and your friends and family have given you everything to try to make that dream a reality, or would you rather hear it now? So that's my advice, get out there, get out there and get heard. Your friends and family are always going to tell you it is amazing, so get out there and get feedback, if you can.

Catherine: Absolutely, so they need somebody like you who will tell them that cold hard truth before they get too far into it. That can save them a lot of heartaches, a lot of money, a lot of stress, a lot of everything.

Sherry: Yes, yes. Most entrepreneurs tell me, "I wish I'd known about you a year ago." That's so true.

Catherine: I can see that.

Sherry: You've got to understand as an entrepreneur too that we're not here to harm you. We want you to be successful, but we're also going to tell you the truth because we watch this day in and day out. We look at over 100 deals, just my group. We look at over 100 deals a month to find seven that we feel can present to a deal screening to find the four that can come in the forum, but at least you can be seen and have the committees look at you and have all the preprocessor to look at, before you go to the actual forum and are ready. You just take the advice, and the number one thing I look for in a C.E.O. is, are you coachable, do you take the information from people who know what they're doing and at least come back with a proposal that says, "I don't agree with you here's why", "That's fine", or "Yes, I like what you said and here's what we're going to do about it."? We're not saying you have to yield and do exactly what we asked, but you have to have some logic for what you are doing and why and we don't have to agree.

Catherine: Right. What kind of advice would you have for somebody to help them to become more coachable?

Sherry: Listen, just listen. Take the feedback; mull it around and see if it makes sense to you. Not all feedback is good feedback; you know we all have our opinions. If I could tell the entrepreneurs that when we do a deal screening and we go around the room, there are three categories: there is allow the company to come to the forum; there's the delay, meaning there is something they have to fix before we see them again; or there's the deny, meaning we don't want anything to do with this company. In a room of forty people, you will get allow, allow, delay, deny, allow, delay…. Not everybody agrees with what is good and what is bad, that's why you want to get in front of more people. So don't just go to one angel investor and say, "How is this?" because they might love it, and then you go to the next ten, and they're like, " Yeah, no."

Catherine: Excellent.

Sherry: Did I answer your question?

Catherine: Yes, you did, thank you. I think the keyword, as you said, is to be willing to listen. That's where being coachable begins.

Sherry: Right, and again, don't just be steamrolled. Just listen and then if you totally in your heart disagree, have a reason and have an answer but don't be too stuck on your product that you don't listen to the experts because most these investors have been investing for awhile. An average investor invests in five deals a year, so they know, and they see their money go out the window many many times. So the average individual invests in five companies a year. They have experience. We joke that the reason that the members are members of Keiretsu is that we can save them from a bad deal, that's just as important as getting a good deal. I can save them from being burned by a bad deal, and that means something to them.

Catherine: Absolutely. Fabulous! That was a lot of great information, and I can see how your company does some great things and I really I love the process that you take these businesses through in helping them to get started and maybe, more importantly, helping them to make sure they're on the right path so that they don't make a lot of mistakes that many businesses do make.

Sherry: Yes, yes.

Catherine: Well, thank you.

Sherry: Yeah, I appreciate it, thank you so much!

CHAPTER 16

Wally and Melody Fosmore

Owners- Fosmore Construction

A person who never made a mistake never tried anything new.
~ Albert Einstein

Catherine: Welcome, we have a unique and special guest today. As a matter of fact, it's not just one guest, but it's two guests. Today we have a couple that works together as a husband and wife team for Fosmore Construction. Wally and Melody Fosmore, the owners of Fosmore construction.

Wally started Fosmore construction in 2004 because he is passionate about high-quality construction and remodeling and has since grown a satisfied group of customers through word of mouth referrals. Wally is a journey level electrician and a certified HVAC technician and welder. He has worked on multimillion dollar projects as a facility manager for the local community colleges and has worked with numerous architects and engineers. He loves to build and, more importantly, loves knowing their company is improving the lives of their clients.

Melody has always had a knack for creativity and over twenty years has worked as a graphic designer for several companies. She has an eye for de-tail and color and loves to collaborate with clients who need a little help discovering the best bit fit of fixtures, tile, wall color and other elements that contribute to an overall living space. Melody is an accomplished textile quilt artist. She takes great satisfaction in working with Wally to bring quality design, construction resources, and experience to their client's lives.

Melody and Wally together have three sons and four grandchildren that they are very excited about. They have lived in the same neighborhood in Shoreline, Washington for over thirty years. They thought that would just be a little fun fact to share.

Wally and melody welcome. I am so delighted to have the both of you on my show today, and it's such an honor to be able to have a couple of teams to learn from.

Wally & Melody: Thank you very much. It's fun to be here.

Catherine: Wonderful. You had shared with me that you've lived in the same neighborhood for over 30 years, though not necessarily in the same house that's very intriguing.

Melody: Well we bought our first house on one street and raised two children there. We had two kids eleven and a half months apart and then two kids thirteen years apart, so we did it every way that you shouldn't have your children. When our third child came, the house became instantly too small, but because our older boys were getting ready to go to college in two years, we thought that we would stay put and maybe remodel. Ironically, we weren't able to make that happen (this was before we started the business) so we found a house a block and half away that was big enough for everybody and then we moved. Of course, as soon as we moved one of our sons got married and moved away, and the other one left as well, so we had a house that was way too big and we've been there ever since.

Catherine: When your children started to grow up and move out did you then move back to another house in the neighborhood or are you still in the same place?

Melody: We stayed. We actually have the business in the lower half of the house, so that's a convenient place to host the business office for our growing team, but it won't be long before we need to relocate our business, so we will probably rent out the bottom half of the house (it's a separate living space with a kitchen, bedrooms, living room and all that) so we'll be able to do something different with the house. We will probably stay here until we're old.

Catherine: Excellent. Tell us about your construction business. How did the two of you decide to go into construction and how did you go about starting your business?

Wally: Well, I had worked in education facilities management for some years. I started out with Ketchikan school district and worked in their facilities then I moved down here to Seattle. Melody and I met shortly after that. My background is mostly on the commercial side and on the owner's side of that. I would sit across the table from the contractors instead of being on the contractor side. I was the owner's representative for capital projects for a couple of community colleges for a 20 - 23 year period or thereabouts. I had thought about starting a business many years ago and just never did. I was on a trajectory working for the community colleges and eventually with budget reductions and other things it was becoming increasingly challenging, and it wasn't fun anymore. When I left there, I decided to start a company. Initially, the thought was to...because of my background would be more on the commercial side, but it seemed that following the leads and developing projects was initially with people that we knew it sort of just mostly stayed on the residential side. It was exciting to have the prospect of running my company instead of being part of a much larger organization - working more directly with clients and accomplishing the work.

Catherine: When you started out, did you both create this business together or was it something, Wally, that you started and then brought Melody in at a later point in time?

Melody: Wally loves to share everything with me whether I want to know about it or not and so basically throughout the years that were together I learned a lot about everything he knew about so when he started the company I was kind of trained about what construction was all about, but at the time that he started I was actually going to school to get my graphic design degree. I was just finishing it up, and our oldest son got married, and I was already getting my education but also doing freelance work on the side and my clients wanted more of my time, so I kept doing my graphic design work independent of Wally. In the evenings I got to hear about everything and I would help him as I could with various things like bookkeeping, which I had no business doing.

Wally: Initially it was just me, and I hired some carpenters here and there to work with me. For awhile we had two halftime employees, and then we just kept adding staff as the project size and complexity grew. Melody kind of jumped in with both feet about four or five years ago.

Melody: About four years ago Wally got a herniated disc, and then he got a great massage that made it worse. He was literally on his back for three weeks with his feet up in the air. That was the only way he could be in any comfortable position to not experience excruciating pain while we waited for the surgery date. The week that that happened we had signed two new contracts for two new jobs, and we had another third big one in the wings; they were ready to go. At that time we had already gone through the recession and

Wally had survived the recession by continuing his networking. He would hang out in the aisles of Lowes and Home Depot and overhear the people having conversations with the staff, and as soon as he figured out the staff didn't know what they were talking about, he waited for them to leave and then he would go to help the people.

Wally: I provided free coaching.

Melody: Yeah, he did free coaching but sometimes it turned into a contract, and I think he got a couple of jobs that way, but the other thing that he did was he worked with a flipper who flipped homes, and he got a lot of good training on the job.

Wally: It turned into a good opportunity because the real estate developer that we were working with was trained as an architect. I would look at properties before they bought them and talked about the possibilities. I would do a structural assessment and talk about what the optimal result might be and then she could make up the drawings. It wasn't like some of the flipping shows you see on T.V. Where they just clean it up and put a coat of paint on it. We were moving walls and leveling houses and new roads, new windows, new kitchens, and bathrooms; they were significant projects.

Melody: When we figured out that her main way of making business was to keep us from making any money we realized the relationship had to end. About that time the recession was coming to an end, and we were getting more business. We got some nice jobs, and we added to our staff. So about the time that Wally's back went out, we hired a new guy that was really skilled as a carpenter and he knew as much as Wally did about a bunch of stuff, so that was the direction we wanted to go where we would hire somebody equal to or better than Wally and then we could release him to run a job and not have Wally have to be doing everything on all the job sites.

Wally: That way we could run multiple jobs.

Melody: His back then went out and so the week that we started these two new jobs and had all this business coming in the door, he was unable to work. Our guys were making the best of it, but I had to be Wally which meant that I had to bring the computer upstairs and while he was on pain meds he talked me through building a budget for a big job and then I created the contract which I had never done before. I learned how to drive his sprinter truck and get the materials and deliver them all over town to the different job sites. I did dump runs, I met with the clients, I met with the staff, I dealt with everything, and then Wally would help me as he could, but he was in a lot of pain. By the time he got done with his surgery which was about a month time of him being out of commission, it had become a friendly takeover, and I was fully engaged; I enjoyed it, and I didn't want to let go.

So there was a little of a tussle between us about who was doing what and we figured that out, but we also were working with a great coach who was helping us. We had already been working with him individually and then together he really started working intensely with us about how to manage that and how to listen to each other and how to be better players together, how to be kind to each other, how to take time off, how to separate our work from our relationship, you know we have a work relationship and we have a...like it's husband versus business partner and so forth, but we received some support and helped that way which was great. That was probably the biggest change because we were doubling our sales that year just by people wanting more work but then when we joined forces and worked on our roles and developed our team, we doubled our sales again the next year and this year we're doubling our sales again. So we've had intense growth which is always a challenge.

Wally: The challenge is managing so that we don't grow too fast. That was one of our goals or my goals, to begin with. I wanted...if I was going to make a mistake I wanted it to be a small mistake, not a big mistake because we saw a lot of companies that went out of business during the recession and we didn't really realize that until we advertised for a lead carpenter position and got 80 applicants and about 60 of the applicants had run their own businesses and had lost them. It was pretty surprising that that was the dismal state of the market and we just didn't even know it was that bad.

Melody: We were survivors, and we didn't know it. We just ended up...not to say that's it's been all rosy...we've made tons of mistakes; we're still making them every day. Our goal is the way we run our company with our staff is we create an environment where this is a no blame safe zone because everybody is so concerned about covering their you know what because they don't want to be holding the freight for the mistake, and the general contractor tends to be the one holding the freight because the client doesn't want to pay the bill and the sub-contractor doesn't want to pay the bill and certainly the vendor doesn't want to pay the bill, so it ends up being the General Contractor. Internally, in our staff in our office when we have a team meeting we do not allow people to blame or shame anybody else on the staff and if they've made a mistake we try to make it comfortable enough for them to own it.

Wally: We try to make it so that anytime there's a mistake or an error made, even if it's a wrong cut, there's a learning opportunity. Quite often we'll bring that up in staff meeting which we have every week. We start out the week every Monday with the whole crew here in the office, and we do lookaheads for developing work, we work on budgets and budget development for projects as well as technical and safety reminders.

Melody: We like the staff to have a voice in the company. We work hard to give everybody a time to talk and a time to weigh in and so there's a lot of collaboration because we have a good staff. A lot of our guys are older, and so they've got a well of knowledge that's wonderful for everybody to learn from what they might have done or what they think is right. Of course, if we start talking about cars or fishing then all of a sudden we've got to end that part of the conversation, but we do enjoy each other so the meetings are fun and that's great. We take care of our guys; we take care of all of our staff. We've walked through some cancers and some other serious illnesses with our staff, and they walked with us through our stuff, and so there's a bond of connection. I would say we're kind of like family, but I wouldn't imagine they'd want to come to our house for Christmas; nonetheless, we do care for them. On weekends, if we need to, we'll spend the time to connect with somebody if they need help. One of our guys had a severe kidney infection earlier this year, and he was on his back for a week, and meanwhile his roof was half done, and all the guys were ready to jump in and go that weekend to fix it for him and when we told him that, we said, "Hey we're ready to come and finish your roof," he refused because he's in that way but nonetheless it was indicative to me that everybody was willing and able to go and I thought that it was really great.

Catherine: That's incredible! I hear a lot of great things that are clearly attributing to your success and I gather the most important piece of this is the way that you work with your staff as a team, the way that you treat them and connect and care for them, and also the way the two of you have learned to work together as a couple. I'm glad that you brought that up because one of the questions that I had for you is how do you manage to work together as husband and wife and to have that personal relationship as well as having that business relationship. I know there are a lot of people - husbands and wives that try to go into business together and they just don't know how to work those pieces together or separately per se. I hear some people say, "Oh my gosh I could never work with my spouse, that just wouldn't work; we would drive each other nuts!"

Melody: Right, and a lot of that comes down to control doesn't it? We are older, so we've been weathered by a lot of issues. As you go through a marriage there are tons of opportunities to say, "I'm done with this joker, I'm out of here." We have… well mainly Wally, because of Wally we've weathered the storm, he's pretty steady.

Wally: Well, back to your question - I think that we have complementary skills and so the organizational skills and team building and things that Melody has brought into focus with the growth of the company is something that I wouldn't have done; it's not something I would have even thought about in some cases, so we have complementary skills. Also, when Melody came into the business out of necessity while I was injured, I think that she learned quite a lot more about what it was that I did every day and she got a better understanding of the breadth of what it took to take a project from planning through completion.

Melody: Yeah, I used to get frustrated with him because he wasn't home at a specific time or we didn't make any money on the project and I would ask, "Why not? You told me it was going to be this long, but it's not." I would be too frustrated, but I just didn't understand, and now I do. I think there is something about working together that gives you an opportunity to see life from your spouse's perspective. If you have staff it's almost like having kids again because you know that they're listening to you when you're talking to your spouse, so you have to be respectful, and I think when you practice respectfulness it starts becoming a habit and then you are. There's a lot to be said for having an accountable eye on you and your life throughout each day where you realize that every word that comes out of your mouth is being observed and as a leader, you're setting a course; you're setting an example.

Wally: You have to set the tone. The another thing that we haven't talked about that's been, I guess, a differentiator for us from other companies in the market because everyone has heard a bad story about a contractor that took the money and ran or did poor work and covered it up or something like that, is that we set a really high standard for treating our clients well. We had a meeting last night with a client couple that we've done three previous projects for. In fact, the first project I did for them was almost ten years ago. Once we're working with a client, it's not uncommon that we're their contractor for life because we care, and it's evident we care, from their home as if it was our own. We set high standards that way, and that's the reason that we were able to survive and grow while a lot of other companies were withering away.

Melody: We also didn't overextend ourselves. We probably were one of few people that when the mortgage company said, "Hey just tell us how much you make, we don't care, we're not going to check it out. Just leave a number, just go ahead." I thought, "Oh my gosh, I mean you've got to be out of your mind! You've got to know how much I make; this is ridiculous." So I didn't do the loan. We just didn't overextend ourselves. I can't say that we were wise and smart but by not being greedy, I guess, we didn't overextend ourselves; nonetheless, I think that surviving the recession is one thing, making the most of the boom that we're in right now is going to be another test and a roadblock, if you will, in front of us because growing so fast has put a lot of strain on us personally. We're not young anymore; it's hard work, and we're tired all the time. We've had to learn how to take breaks and how to honor our relationship and our lives with more work breaks as much as we can so we started taking three-day weekends here and there; we started going out with friends more; we started to engage each other in kayaking, walking, camping, or hiking as much as we possibly can because those things can give us life and energize us. I'm not saying we do it all the time, but we do it as much as we can. Seeing our grandkids, of course, is another way.

Catherine: You've mentioned a couple of times that the roadblocks haven't ended; they don't go away; you don't get to a certain point in your life or a certain point in your business where you're done, and you get over the road-blocks, and it's just smooth sailing from here on out.

Melody: There's no graduation from that. That's why it's so important to be coachable and allow that every day there is going to be a problem. Rather than going, "Oh my gosh every day is going to be a problem," it's like, "Okay, every day there's going to be a problem, so how are we going to meet it? What's the best way to meet it? Is it something that can be fixed right away or does we need to table it and deal with it as a group?" We just kind of triage it. I am on the front line and sometimes when a client is upset with us, with the company, I get to hear about it. I am the front line of the discouragement or unhappiness that sometimes comes up with clients because maybe we've blown it or maybe there's been an upsetting situation in their life; it's really nice to be able to come back to the office and have that supportive environment where the staff is saying, "Wow, what do you know what do you need right now? What can you do to be kind to yourself right now? They can feel that way, but it's not defining you as a person." We've actually learned as a team to not put our clients down in the office because it just creates this negative environment and it's better to just continue that level of respect as much as we can to say, "Alright, so this person must have had a bad day; that's why they're a jerk on the phone." The whole idea is that we try to be a little more graceful in how we treat each other and our clients because, you know, we're all in it together here.

Wally: Even with our clients, we work in partnership, and we start out the projects that way. In our first meeting, we talk about the fact that this is going to be a partnership; that we're going to help them through the decision processes. We're just real clear about what our role is, what we need from them regarding decisions, and that we can encourage them how to make good decisions and point out what the possibilities are because it can be more than a little bit intimidating. We do this a lot but when someone comes on... we had a client a few years ago where we were doing a kitchen remodel, and she understood that that was the day and when we got there she wasn't quite ready and there were still dishes in the sink and the dishwasher....

Melody: She was in a little bit of a denial.

Wally: She was a little unrealistic about what demolition really meant and so she got a late start, went to work, then came home that afternoon and we had very carefully taken care of all the dishes and got everything saved and then proceeded to put up the dust walls, tear out all the cabinets and all the demolition was done by the time she got home. She walked in and looked at the place and burst into tears because she just wasn't ready emotionally and thought that we had just blown her house to bits. This trust relationship is very important to establish and to maintain throughout the project, and she just needed a shoulder to cry on as she looked at her house.

Melody: Catherine, you've used the word success a lot in your questions and me really kind of almost laugh when I hear the word success, because even though we may be growing, I do not feel successful. I don't really know what that means; this may be one of those times in life where you're just doing the best you can and hanging on and doing what you know you should do and work as hard as you can, and then you look back and go, "Wow, I just sailed around the world, and I didn't know it."

It's like one of those times where I don't know what the next year or two or three will hold for us. We can have a strategy and a roadmap; we can plan all we want but only God knows, right? We're just going to do what we can do. We're going to do the best we can, but anything can happen. All we can do, all I have personally that I can do every day, is the very best that I can do and to be the best person I can be every day and sometimes I don't; I fail; I fall; sometimes I'm not a nice person. I think that that's the only thing any of us can do. I think that construction has, in a lot of cases, a negative connotation for a lot of people because they think that we're out to get them and the truth is a lot of people are out to get us. They want us to help pay for their project. We really come to it every time with a view that this is a partnership and it is potentially a wonderful experience. There are many of them that we hold on to and we've been lucky to have some great clients to work with. We feel blessed for that reason, but we also know that we're dealing with all kinds of people and all kinds of circumstances. Everybody comes to the table with their bag of hurts and conditions that they're working from. Sometimes this takes a lot of psychology to deal with people.

Wally: Sometimes we end up doing the marital counseling for the clients because they see things differently about what they want to end up with and so we have to kind of walk through that process.

Melody: We've brought meals, and we've brought care packages and things to people when things are at the very worst and they've just had it, and there's no end in sight. We know it's coming to an end, but they don't so we do what we can in that way to help.

Wally: That usually happens when we're far enough into the project when the mechanicals and the electrical and things are all to completion and then sheetrocking happens and then it's almost like adding salt to injury for the client even though it's pretty short lived.

Catherine: Well, I would like to say in regards to what you said about success and not knowing what the definition of success is and what I hear from you is that success is something that's ever evolving. You have many things that you've come up against, many things that you've overcome, many things that you have accomplished and in those moments there has been a success. In each of those moments, the success may be different. As things continue to evolve for you and continue to grow and you continue to have other challenges that may come up, like you said you don't know what could happen tomorrow, but as those things happen because of what you have created for yourself and others, together, you have created this ability to take whatever it is that will come your way, and you will work through it; you will be successful, whatever that looks like.

Wally: I guess I think of success more as a trajectory, not a destination. It's just something that you may, as Melody mentioned, look back and see where things have changed and there has been an improvement or success in other words, but it's more of a trajectory to me that takes place over a period. It's not just winning a race or something. Every one of our projects come to a successful conclusion but over a period we're moving into new projects, we're completing projects, developing new and training up the staff and so it's just kind of a general direction to me, not just a destination that says, "Okay, we've won the race."

Melody: I appreciate what you were saying, Catherine. You need to find success at the moment because there is no grand finale on any of this. Here we are little ol' ma and pa Fosmore in Shoreline, Washington. We're just running a small company, doing a small business compared to a lot of other people that have done some pretty amazing things with their lives. We are both healthy; our kids are okay. We have our sorrows but we don't have any massive Grand Canyon sized splits in our lives that we have to overcome, so I feel very grateful for the opportunity to do what we get to do.

Wally: We have nine people working in our company and I think every single person enjoys the completion of the project or thinking back about what we've done, what we started out with, the problems that we were challenged with, and the nice part about that is that when we're done with a project we've changed the way, someone, in a lot of cases, the way they think about or live in their home and in some cases we've changed the way they think about their life because of how we changed their home. It's more than just the finishes; it's how we've enabled them to have a different perspective about their lives because of the way their home is, and they can entertain or share with family, and it's more comfortable or safe, or all of those things.

Catherine: There has been a lot of success that you have reached and seen in the last several years as you've built this business. Success is in the eye of the beholder. You get to decide what success is for you. I just want to finish by thanking you both. I have enjoyed this opportunity to speak with the both of you. This is the first time that I have interviewed with a couple or with a team like the two of you, and I enjoyed it. I love all the information and tips that you have shared. You've given a lot of great information for others to glean from and use in their lives and their businesses to be able to create the success that they're looking for. So again, thank you, Wally and Melody.

Wally & Melody: Well, thank you very much and good luck to you on all that you're doing.

Made in the USA
Charleston, SC
06 February 2017